COPYRIGHT STATEMENT:

DEDICATION

To my reckless, feckless, feral and adventurous elder brother Adam (ENTP): who walked by my side for the first 14.5 years of my life. You did and said whatever burned within you. You scared the hell out of me! But you were the most alive person I've ever met.

"Knowing yourself is the beginning of all wisdom."

Aristotle

CONTENT

PREAMBLE

This book is a dream come true for me. It is a book I have been metaphorically writing all my life. It is the book I have always aspired to write.

It is the book that I most wished I could have read as a young man with my adult life still lying in front of me.

I believe the personality theory first introduced by Sigmund Freud and developed further by Erik Erikson and Carl Jung has had more positive impact on our world than any other psychological theory.

Certainly, it is the most applied psychology theory, particularly now with the 3 billion-dollar industry of online dating (this is just its worth in the USA), which uses this theory to successfully match people.

When you arrive in this world, no sooner are you consciously aware of your own existence than the world around you demands to know who you are, what you can do and what you want.

Everyone you meet is to a degree listless in your company until they know the answers to these three questions. Without knowing this, they do not know what type of relationship they want with you.

All relationships are based on trust and mutuality i.e. What can I do for you? What can you do for me? Is what we can do for each other of equal worth? And, do I believe in you?

Until you know who you are, you cannot truly be yourself or truly believe in yourself. Therefore, you cannot be fully congruent. Any degree of incongruence is sensed by others and decreases their trust and confidence in you. This adversely affects the quality of all your relationships, intimate, social and business. Consequently, your efficacy and the quality of your life experience reduces. It is the quality of relationships, which underpins all human success and determines your degree of influence and effectiveness.

Conversely, when you truly know yourself, accept yourself, you can truly be yourself. Be completely congruent, confident and comfortable. When you are comfortable with yourself, other people are comfortable with you. You know what you like, don't like, what your strengths, weaknesses are. You manage yourself effectively. Consequently, you know what you can do to help others and you know what you need from others.

People look to you for answers about you. If you accept yourself as you are, others will accept you as you are also. If you value yourself and your opinions, others will value you and your opinions.

When you are congruent, you recognise others who are congruent, and you will be attracted towards each other due to the trust, automatically generated.

You will know the type of person your ideal romantic partner needs to be. As you will know whose life you can enhance and who can enhance yours.

You will know what career fits you best, as you will know where you can add most value and you will know what challenge is required to maximise your own personal growth.

The benefits of this self-knowledge are incalculable.

However, the journey to achieve this self-knowledge is a road that's neither an easy or a short one.

This book aims to expedite this journey somewhat, through making complex psychological theory simple and delivering critical knowledge in the most rapid way possible.

INTRODUCTION

"No one, but yourself can know who you are. Finding who you are is to know what music to dance to. Once you know this, you can LOSE YOURSELF in the DANCE of LIFE!" Mark Joseph

"On holiday in Utah, USA, where most of my family live, I learned that sometimes you have to climb a mountain in order to get a different perspective!"

Growing up as an INFJ personality type, people would tell me I was from another planet!   Occasionally I would think, "Is there something wrong with me?" When I discovered personality theory, it was an absolute revelation because I felt validated! I understood why people thought I was from another planet!

It was because my brain was wired differently to 99% of the population. But that's O.K, I have strengths that few others have, and I am not alone, there are other people like me in the world.

This book may be for some, the start of an exciting journey. And this journey begins with a question.

The most important question you will ever ask yourself: 'Who am I?'

Why? Because until you know the answer to this question, you will not have the clarity necessary to generate purpose in your life. To know who you are, is to know what you like and don't like; to know what you want and don't want.

Getting to know yourself is a journey and understanding your personality is the best place to start, as it will make you aware of your hardwired preferences i.e. the traits you cannot change, so need to accept and embrace. Thus, illuminating your innate strengths and weaknesses.

Weaknesses are just your strengths inverted. So, accept them and confidently display them. Your transparent vulnerability endears people to you. Consequently, they will accept you for who you are and accommodate you.

As you focus on your strengths you will grow in confidence and as you increase the transparency of your weaknesses you will grow in humility. You will attract those who can help you with your weaknesses and you will meet those who you can help with your strengths.

Do not fear becoming your true self, you have nothing of real value to lose, only your mental chains, and a fulfilled life to gain.

Once you accept it is O.K to be who you truly are, you will by default be accepting your unique mission and purpose. You will inadvertently, be giving others the permission to accept themselves and unleashing an irrepressible force for good into this world i.e. your innate inner passion.

It was this personality theory information that really changed my life for the better. People say, 'knowledge is power' and it's not. What is powerful however is relevant knowledge that is applied in an intelligent manner. When I learnt this personality information, it helped me to know who I truly was and to fully accept myself. My inner confidence grew exponentially. What followed was my job turned into a career as I knew the direction I wanted to take, and I identified passionate hobbies for life. My main hobby being writing self-help psychology books and coaching self-development.

It was an increased understanding of my personality traits that helped me identify my strength for writing and coaching. INFJs tend to be more adept at writing than verbal communication. Also, INFJs are innately the most driven to help others achieve their full potential and we perform best in one to one situations.

I became the 'master of my own destiny.' Discovering my balance in life. I found I had more energy for my career as I followed my passion of writing and coaching in my private life.

To you, the reader: enjoy this exciting adventure of self-discovery and feel free to contact me and let me know how this book helps you or to request personality & character development coaching.

"The two most important days in your life are the day you are born and the day you find out why."

Mark Twain

I have noticed that there are quite a few personality tests around on the internet now. Many of the popular ones are focussing more on a few 'traits or behaviours' that correlate with monetary success predictors. I think any increase in self-knowledge is valuable. However, I believe the personality theory I will share with you in this book to be the most valuable that I have seen for the following reasons:

1. It is based on the theory developed by the life-long work and research of the Swiss psychiatrist, Carl Jung, the 'Father of Analytical Psychology.' One of the greatest minds and influencers to have ever lived

2. It doesn't focus solely on the trite correlators with success. Be aware that those type of tests, to some greater

> or lesser extent have defined success in some measurable way, usually money or fame as these are the easiest ways to measure and the most alluring.
>
> 3. Genuine personality theory focusses on one thing, the way our brains are wired, and how that effects our preferences in relation to our focus, thinking, beliefs, values, likes, dislikes, strengths and weakness

Once you truly understand yourself, what makes you tick, what you enjoy, what your innate strengths are, you will instinctively bring greater value to humanity.

What the world needs most is you to be you. Becoming your true self, means living a fulfilled life, this is the only meaningful definition of success for me, and it can't be measured.

The personality theory that I am sharing with you in this book, is in my opinion the most comprehensive. It is also the one that most effectively promotes both self-development and the quality and efficacy of all your relationships.

CHAPTER 1: RAPID PERSONALITY TEST

"The better you know yourself, the better your relationship with the rest of the world." Toni Collette

Only you can work out what personality type you are.

You do this through self-reflection and introspection.

Answering the following questions honestly is a start to this self-reflective process.

Pic 1 – group study - I feel energised in a group of people

"I feel uncomfortable when I am on my own. I am seen as social and outgoing. I feel comfortable speaking in a group. In fact, I love speaking out loud, it helps me make sense of my thoughts and I learn what others think of them. I feel comfortable when meeting new people and have lots of friends and aquaintances."

How much does the above statement accurately describe you? Score yourself 1-10. 1 being nothing like you, and 10 being an accurate description.

1. Record your score out of 10:______

Pic 2 – Downtime on your own - Time to reflect and think

"Leading a group discussion or speaking in a group takes a lot of energy. I need regular downtime by myself, to take it easy, relax, re-energise, reflect and think.

I prefer to have just a few close friends. I get energised by my inner world of thoughts, ideas and reflections."

How much does the above statement accurately describe you? Score yourself 1-10. 1 being nothing like you, and 10 being an accurate description.

2. Record your score out of 10:_______

Pic 3 – Original ideas that change the future

How excited would you be to come up with a unique idea or theory that would have a big impact on the future world?

Score 1-10 your level of excitement. 1 being not really interested and 10 being the most exciting thing in the world.

3. Record your score out of 10:_______

Pic 4 – Highly observant skills and an eye for detail

"I am very observant and switched on? I am always aware of what is going on around me at any given time. I am always present, in the here and now in this moment? It is very difficult to distract me or to get my mind to wonder off into a dreamland? Not much gets passed me!"

How much does the above statement accurately describe you? Score yourself 1-10. 1 being nothing like you, and 10 being an accurate description.

4. Record your score out of 10:________

Pic 5 – Emotional impact on others

"People would describe me as sensitive towards other people's feelings. How my words and actions affect others is most important to me. I would avoid at all costs hurting someone else's feelings. I find it difficult and often unnecessary to tell someone I disagree with them."

How well does this statement describe you? Score yourself 1-10. 1 being nothing like you, and 10 being an accurate description.

5. Record your score out of 10:_______

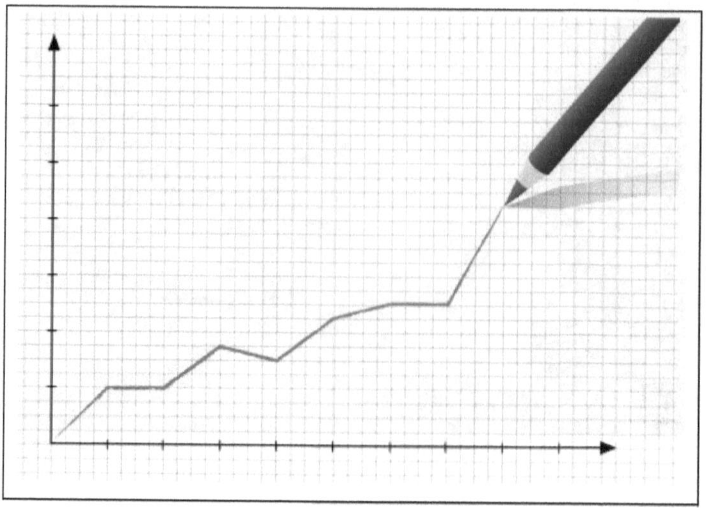

Pic 6 – facts rule

"I prefer to make my decisions based on what is just, factual and logical. I don't shy away from challenging or correcting people if they misrepresent the facts."

How well does this statement describe you? Score yourself 1-10. 1 being nothing like you, and 10 being an accurate description.

6. Record your score out of 10:_______

Task list

- ✓ 1. Agree all holidays for next year
- ✓ 2. Book dog sitter
- ✓ 3. Book holiday package deals
- ✓ 4. Book transport to airport
- ✓ 5. Get holiday insurance
- ✓ 6. Book holiday dates at work
- ✓ 7. Tell family holiday dates
- ✓ 8. Renew passports

Pic 7 – Life ordered & under control

"I feel so much better now my list of tasks is complete. I prefer it when everything is decided and in order?"

How well does this statement describe you? Score yourself 1-10. 1 being nothing like you (this list makes you feel ucomfortable as it is too restrictive), and 10 being an accurate description as you like everything in your life to be decided, ordered and in control.

7. Record your score out of 10:_______

Pic 8 – highly flexible & adaptable

"I am completely flexible, last minute changes are exciting. Am always ready to adapt plans. Just don't want to miss out on an exciting opportunity. I wait to last minute to make a final decision to ensure no better option comes to light."

How well does this statement describe you? Score yourself 1-10. 1 being nothing like you, and 10 being an accurate description.

8. Record your score out of 10:_______

Record your scores from each pic in the table below and for each score times it by 10 to get your % score for that specific preference.

Preference pairs explanation	Pic	**Preference pairs**		x10 = % Extravert	x10 = % Introvert
		Extravert (E)	Introvert (I)		
Energy focus external or internal world	1				
	2				

	Pic	iNtuitive (N)	Sensor (I)	x10 = % iNtuitive	x10 = % Sensor Score
Gathering information 5 senses or intuition	3				
	4				

	Pic	Thinker (T)	Feeler (F)	x10 = % Thinker Score	x10 = % Feeler Score
Decision making fact-based or human feelings impact	5				
	6				

	Pic	Judger (J)	Perceiver (P)	x10 = % Judger Score	x10 = % Perceiver
Interaction with world structured or flexible	7				
	8				

We all use each of these 8 preferences (identified in the table above), just like right-handed people use both their right and left hands. However out of the pairs we will usually favour one more than the other.

1	E	Energised by their external world / social interaction
2	I	Energised most by their internal world / alone time
3	S	Focuses on what & how: tasks of here and now, concrete facts & reality
4	N	Focuses on why & what if: abstract, ideas and future possibilities
5	F	Makes decisions according to personal values & impact on other's feelings
6	T	Makes decisions according to objective facts
7	J	Wants things planned, structured, settled, decided, trusts established process & authority
8	P	Wants things open, spontaneous, free to capitalise on best opportunity, challenge established process & authority to see if there's a better way

The preference from each pair, which you scored highest forms your personality type acronym. There are 16 types of personality types in the table below, each with a one-word descriptor. Please tick the one you think you are. Bear in mind your decision may change as you learn more about each personality type and yourself.

Defenders - SJs	Adventurers - SPs
Supervisor (ESTJ)	Promoter (ESTP)
Inspector (ISTJ)	Crafter (ISTP)
Provider (ESFJ)	Performer (ESFP)
Protector (ISFJ)	Composer (ISFP)
Dreamers - NFs	**Investigators - NTs**
Teacher (ENFJ)	Fieldmarshall (ENTJ)
Counsellor (INFJ)	Mastermind (INTJ)
Champion (ENFP)	Inventor (ENTP)
Healer (INFP)	Architect (INTP)

The personality group 'Defenders' are usually represented as the colour yellow (dependable). 'Adventurers' as red (risk-takers). 'Dreamers' as green (peaceful) and 'Investigators' as blue (cool-headed).

The table below identifies the % of each psychology group in the world population.

Trait	Group name	Role in society	Population
SJs	Defenders	Duty seekers	45%
SPs	Adventurers	Action seekers	25%
NFs	Dreamers	Ideal seekers	20%
NTs	Investigators	Knowledge seekers	10%

Population %	
Introversion	*20%
Sensing	75%
Thinking - men	67%
Feeling - women	67%
Perceiving	50%

Strongly introverted = 20% but people who require some level of social downtime up to 50%

Carl Jung was the Swiss psychiatrist and psychoanalyst who founded analytical psychology and whose research provided the main knowledge for the personality theory I am sharing in this book. He discovered that personalities could be broadly fit into 4 personality groups: defenders, adventurers, dreamers and investigators.

Defenders (SJ): speak mostly of their duties and responsibilities, of what they can keep an eye on and take good care of, and they're careful to obey the laws, follow the rules, and respect the rights of others.

Dreamers (NJ): speak mostly of what they hope for and imagine might be possible for people, and they want to act in good conscience, always trying to reach their goals without compromising their personal code of ethics.

Adventurers (SP): speak mostly about what they see right in front of them, about what they can get their hands on, and they will do whatever works, whatever gives them a quick, effective payoff, even if they must bend the rules.

Investigators (NT): speak mostly of what new problems intrigue them and what new solutions they envision, and always pragmatic, they act as efficiently as possible to achieve their objectives, ignoring arbitrary rules and conventions if need be.

Have you ever had the sense that someone is intelligent, but in a different way to you? Well Carl Jung identified that there were four types of intellect: Strategy, logistics, diplomacy and tactics. We all use each of these intellect types as part of our rational thinking processes. However, we all have intellect type preferences. Each personality group has a different hierarchy of intellect types, usage preference. This is very important information to be aware of when choosing a career.

For example, if your strongest intellect is not 'logistics' it would not be wise to choose 'air traffic control' as a career.

We have all come across people who are 'ducks-out-of-water' in their jobs, for example, a hotel receptionist or holiday rep whose strongest intellect is not 'diplomacy.' Their direct, sharp, cold demeanour says it all in an instant.

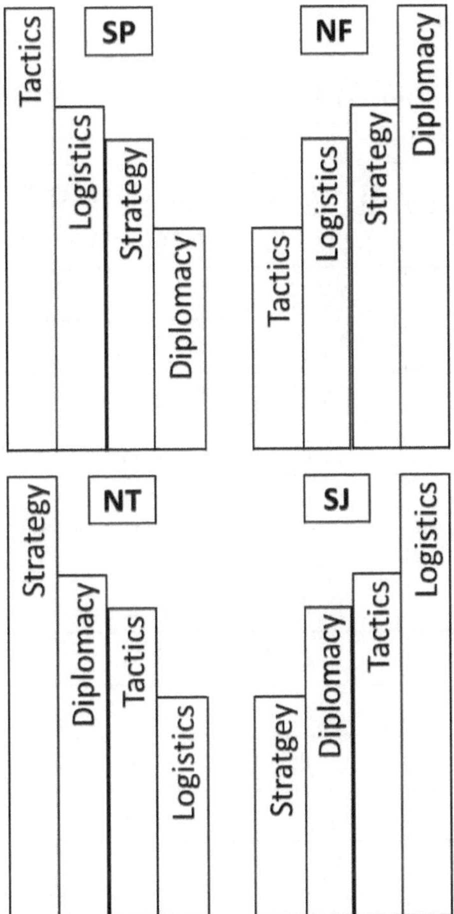

Preferred intellect type usage
Tactics = is the art of making moves to better ones position in the here & now
Logistics = is the procurement, distribution, service & replacement of material goods
Strategy = is identifying the ways & means necessary to achieve a well-defined goal
Diplomacy = is the ability to deal with people in a skilful, tactful (sensitive) manner

Note: diplomacy is more recently been referred to as 'emotional intelligence'

It is also very important knowledge to be aware of when building a team of people to accomplish a specific task. And in deciding which team member(s) are responsible for which tasks or roles within the group.

Look up your personality type in the table below to see what approximate percentage of the world population you represent.

Typing & Population			
Type	Total %	Male %	Female %
ISFJ	13.8	8.1	19.4
ESFJ	12.3	7.5	16.9
ISTJ	11.6	16.4	6.9
ISFP	8.8	7.6	9.9
ESTJ	8.7	11.2	6.3
ESFP	8.5	6.9	10.1
ENFP	8.1	6.4	9.7
ISTP	5.4	8.5	2.4
INFP	4.4	4.1	4.6
ESTP	4.3	5.6	4.3
INTP	3.3	4.8	1.8
ENTP	3.2	4	2.4
ENFJ	2.5	1.6	3.3
INTJ	2.1	3.3	2.1
ENTJ	1.8	2.7	0.9
INFJ	1.46	1.3	1.6

Whatever size of the population your personality type represents, whether you represent the largest group or the smallest, everyone is unique. Why? Well your personality typing might mean you are represented by 8% of the population, for example. But an analysis of your set of strengths and weaknesses will reduce that to perhaps 0.08%. Then, if you, account for your culture; your individual experiences and learnt skills, you become completely unique. No one that has been born or ever will be born, will be exactly-the-same as you.

If your personality forms a large percent of the population, it does so due to evolution: the drive for survival of the human species i.e. your brain is wired with a purpose that is so important to the survival of the species that it requires a large head count to fulfil it.

If your personality type is one that forms a small part of the population, it is also due to evolution: the drive for survival of the human species i.e. your brain is wired with a purpose that is like a back-up plan, when the majority of the population might have got it wrong.

I will give you an example. Across all animal species (including humans) approximately 20% are classed as 'hypersensitive.' This is due to evolution, as it maximises the chance of species survival.

Think about it, when you feed goldfish, 80% of the fish will rush to the surface to grab what they can as fast as they can, to survive. However, 20% of the fish will hang back, they are nervous about rushing towards the dangers of the surface, and the hand that feeds them. They wait for the food to drop well below the frenzy before they feed.

And, if this surface feeding turns out to be a trap and a predator attacks and decimates the 80% population, the remaining 20% can preserve and propagate the species.

CHAPTER 2: PSYCHOLOGICAL PREFERENCES

"Always remember, you are unique, just like everyone else." Margaret Mead

There are four pairs of psychological preferences. The first pair of psychological preferences is Extraversion & Introversion.

Where do you put your attention and get your energy? Do you like to spend time in the outer world of people and things (Extraversion), or in your inner world of ideas and images (Introversion)?

Extraversion and Introversion are terms used by Carl Jung to explain different attitudes people have towards directing their inner energy or focus. These words have a meaning in psychology that is different from the way they are used in everyday language.

Everyone spends time extroverting and time introverting. Don't confuse Introversion with shyness or reclusiveness. They are not necessarily the same.

Take a minute to ask yourself which of the following descriptions seems more natural, effortless, and comfortable for you, extraversion or introversion?

Extraversion (E)
I like getting my energy from active participation in lots of activ-

ities. I'm excited by being with people. I like to energise people. I like moving into action and making things happen. I usually feel at home in the world. I usually understand a problem better when I can talk out loud and listen to what others say about it.

The following usually applies to me:

1. I am seen as outgoing or as a people person

2. I feel comfortable in groups and like working in them

3. I have a wide range of friends and know lots of people

4. I sometimes jump too quickly into an activity and don't take enough time to think it over

5. Before I start a project, I sometimes forget to stop and get clear on what I want to do and why

Introversion (I)

I like getting my energy from dealing with the ideas, pictures, memories, and reactions that are inside my head, in my inner world. I often prefer doing things alone or with one or two people I feel comfortable with. I take time to reflect so that I have a clear idea of what I'll be doing when I decide to act. Ideas are almost solid things for me. Sometimes I like the idea of something better than the real thing.

The following usually applies to me:

1. I am seen as reflective or reserved

2. I feel comfortable being alone and like things I can do on my own

3. I prefer to know just a few people well

4. I am prone to spending too much time reflecting and don't move into action quickly enough

5. I sometimes forget to check with the outside world to see if my

ideas really fit the experience

The second pair of psychological preferences is Sensing and Intuition. Do you pay more attention to information that comes in through your five senses (Sensing), or do you pay more attention to the patterns and possibilities that you see in the information you receive (Intuition)?

Everyone spends time Sensing and time using Intuition.

Take a minute to ask yourself which of the following descriptions seems more natural, effortless, and comfortable for you, sensing or intuition?

Sensing (S)
Paying attention to physical reality, what I see, hear, touch, taste, and smell. I'm concerned with what is actual, present, current, and real. I notice facts and I remember details that are important to me. I like to see the practical use of things and learn best when I see how to use what I'm learning. Experience speaks to me louder than words.

The following usually applies to me:
1. I recall events as snapshots of what actually happened
2. I solve problems by looking through the facts until I understand the issue
3. I am practical and look to the 'bottom line'
4. I start with facts and then form a 'big picture'
5. I trust experience first and trust words and symbols less
6. I can pay so much attention to facts, either present or past, that I miss new possibilities

Intuition (N)

I focus more on impressions or the meaning and patterns of the information I get. I would rather learn by thinking a problem through than by hands-on-experience. I am interested in new things and what is possible, so I tend to think more about the future than the present or the past. I like to work with symbols or abstract theories, even if I don't know how I will use them. I remember events more as an impression of what it was like than actual facts or details of what happened.

The following usually applies to me:

1. I remember events by what I read 'between-the-lines' about their meaning
2. I solve problems by leaping between different ideas and possibilities
3. I am interested in doing things that are new and different
4. I like to see the big picture, then to find out the facts
5. I trust impressions, symbols, and metaphors more than what I have experienced
6. Sometimes I focus so much on new possibilities that I forget to make them a reality

This third preference pair describes how you like to make decisions. Do you like to put more weight on objective principles and impersonal facts (Thinking) or do you put more weight on personal concerns and the people involved (Feeling)?

Don't confuse Feeling with emotion. Everyone has emotions about the decisions they make. Also do not confuse Thinking with intelligence.

Everyone uses Thinking for some decisions and Feeling for others. In fact, a person can make a decision using his or her preference, then test the decision by using the other preference to see what might not have been considered.

Take a minute to ask yourself which of the following descriptions seems more natural, effortless, and comfortable for you, feeling or thinking?

Feeling (F)

I feel that I can make the best decisions by weighing what people care about and the points of view of persons involved in a situation. I am concerned with values and what is best for the people involved. I like to do what whatever will establish and maintain harmony. In my relationships I appear caring, warm and tactful.

The following usually applies to me:

1. I have a people or communication orientation
2. I am concerned with harmony and nervous when it is missing
3. I look for what is important to others and express concern for others
4. I make decisions with my heart and want to be compassionate
5. I believe being tactful is more important than speaking the 'cold' truth
6. Sometimes I miss seeing or communicating the hard truth / facts
7. I am sometimes viewed by others as too nice or indirect

Thinking (T)

When I make a decision, I like to find the basic truth or principle to be applied, regardless of the specific situation involved. I like to analyse pros and cons, then be consistent and logical in deciding. I try to be impersonal, so I won't let my personal wishes or other people's wishes influence me.

The following usually applies to me:

1. I enjoy technical or scientific activities where logic is important
2. I notice inconsistencies
3. I look for logical explanations or solutions for everything
4. I make decision with my head and fairness
5. I believe telling the truth is more important than being tactful
2. 6. Sometimes I can miss or overlook the 'people-impact' part of a situation
6. Can be viewed as too transactional, uncaring or indifferent

The fourth preference pair describes how you like to live your outer life--what are the behaviours others tend to see? Do you prefer a more structured and decided lifestyle (Judging) or a more flexible and adaptable lifestyle (Perceiving)? This preference may also be thought of as your orientation to the outer world.

Everyone extraverts some of the time. This pair describes whether you extravert (act in the outer world) when you are making decisions or when you are taking in information.

Some people interact with the outside world when they are taking in information. Whether they use the Sensing preference or the Intuitive preference, they are still interacting in the outside world.

Other people do their interacting when they are making decisions. It doesn't matter whether they are using a Thinking preference or a Feeling preference; they are still interacting in the outside world.

Everyone takes in information some of the time. Everyone makes decisions some of the time. However, when it comes to dealing with the outer world, people who tend to focus on making decisions have a preference for Judging because they tend to like things decided. People who tend to focus on taking in information prefer Perceiving because they like to keep things open until the final decision, in order to get more information.

Sometimes people feel they have both. That is true. The J or P preference only tells which preference the person extraverts (shows in their outer life) i.e. How others see you. One person may feel very orderly/structured (J) on the inside, yet their outer life looks spontaneous and adaptable (P). Another person may feel very curious and open-ended (P) in their inner world, yet their outer life looks more structured or decided (J).

Don't confuse Judging and Perceiving with a person's level of organisation. Either preference can be organised.

Take a minute to ask yourself which of the following descriptions seems more natural, effortless, and comfortable for you, judging or perceiving?

Judging (J)
I use my decision-making judging preference (whether it is 'Feeling' or 'Thinking') in my outer life (what is visible to others). To others, will perceive that I prefer a planned or orderly life. I like to have things settled and organised. I feel more comfortable once decisions have been made. I like to bring life under control, where possible.

The following usually applies to me:
      1. I like things to be decided

2. I appear to be task oriented
3. I like to make lists of things to do
4. I like to get my work done before playing
5. I plan work to avoid rushing just before a deadline
6. Sometimes I focus so much on tasks completion that I miss new information / possibilities

Perceiving (P)

I use my perceiving function (whether it is 'Sensing' or 'Intuition') in my outer life. To others, I appear to prefer a flexible and spontaneous way of life, and I like to understand and adapt to the world rather than organise it. Others see me staying open to new experiences and information.

Since this preference only describes how I interact with my outer world, inside myself I might feel planful or decisive).

('Perceiving' here means a preference for taking in information and does not mean you are perceptive, having a sharp insight into people/events).

The following usually applies to me:

1. I like to remain open to respond and adapt
2. I appear loose and casual. I like to keep plans to a minimum
3. I work in bursts of energy
4. I am stimulated by an approaching deadline
5. Sometimes I stay open to new information so long I miss making decisions when they are needed

Remember, your preferences are a result of the way your brain is wired. Therefore, if any activity in your life requires you to act in a way that is opposite to your preference, then it will take more effort and energy to do so. For example, if your preference is extraversion, and you work on your own too much at work you will feel deprived of socialising and will then spend most of your free time out of your home socialising to compensate i.e. to regain a balance.

These personality preferences can be likened to preferences of handedness i.e. right or left handedness. If you are left-handed you can learn to write effectively with your right hand if you practice for long enough each day, but it will never feel as easy and as comfortable as writing with your left hand.

What I am saying to you is, if you have the knowledge of what your innate preferences are i.e. your natural strengths, why would you choose to serve the world by the over-use of your weaknesses instead of focussing on your natural strengths?

CHAPTER 3: YOUR PERSONALITY TYPE TRAITS

"Comparing yourself to others, to gauge your value, is like comparing a priceless work of art with a completely different priceless work of art, to decide which is worth more. Absolutely pointless."

Your personality type is a result of how your brain is hardwired. Therefore, whichever personality type you are now, you will remain throughout your life.

Your personality type will start to be identifiable from early childhood and will be mostly formed by around the age of 12. Your personality development will pass through stages throughout your life, but I will not cover that in this book.

It is important to remember that the personality traits identified in these tables below are how you are likely viewed by others. Therefore, it is extremely important information, both for your self-awareness and for all your relationships, at work, home and social.

If you take one thing from this personality theory, it is that everybody sees and experiences the world in a different way, and each way is just as valid as another. Once you understand this fact it becomes more natural to respect people from different personality groups, different cultures and walks of life.

	Descriptor	Type - Short Description
ESTP	**Promoter** most fun	Flexible and tolerant, they take pragmatic approach focussed on immediate results. Theories and conceptual explanations bore them -- they want to act energetically to solve the problem. Focus on the here-and-now, spontaneous, enjoy each moment that they can be active with others. Enjoy material comfort and style. Learn best through doing.
ISTP	**Mechanic/Crafter** most pragmatic	Tolerant and flexible, quiet observers until a problem appears, then act quickly to find workable solutions. Analyse what makes things work and readily get through large amounts of data to isolate the core of the practical problems. Interested in cause and effect, organise facts using logical principles, value efficiency.
ESFP	**Entertainer** most generous	Outgoing, friendly, and accepting. Exuberant lovers of life, people, and material comforts. Enjoy working with others to make things happen. Bring common sense and a realistic approach to their work, and make work fun. Flexible and spontaneous, adapt readily to new people annd environments. Learn best by trying a new skill with other people.
ISFP	**Artist** most artistic	Quiet, friendly, sensitive, and kind. Enjoy the present moment, what's going on around them. Like to have their own space and to work within their own time frame. Loyal and committed to their values and to people who are important to them. Dislike disagreements and conflicts, do not force their opinions or values on others.
ENFJ	**Giver/Mentor** most persuasive	Warm, empathetic, responsive, and responsible. Highly attuned to the emotions, needs, and motivations of others. Find potential in everyone, want to help others fulfill their potential. May act as catalysts for individual group growth. Loyal, responsive to praise and criticism. Sociable, facilitate others in a group, and provide inspiring leadership.
INFJ	**Counsellor** most reflective	Quietly forceful, original, and sensitive. Tend to stick to things until they are done. Extremely intuitive about people, and concerned for their feelings. Well-developed value systems which they strictly adhere to. Well-respected for their perserverence in doing the right thing. Likely to be individualistic, rather than leading or following.
ENFP	**Insprirer** most optimistic	Warmly enthusiastic and imaginative. See life as full of possibilities. Make connections between events and information very quickly, and confidently proceed based on the patterns they see. Want a lot of affirmation from others, and readily give appreciation and support. Spontaneous and flexible, often rely on their ability to improvise and their verbal fluency.
INFP	**Healer/Mediator** most idealistic	Idealistic, loyal to their values and to people who are important to them. Want an external life that is congruent (harmonious) with their values. Curious, quick to see possibliities, can be catalysts for implementing ideas. Seek to understand people and to help them fulfifil their potential. Adaptable, flexible, and accepting unless one of their values is threatened.
ENTJ	**Executive** most commanding	Frank, decisive, realists, they assume leadership readily. Quickly see illogical and inefficient procedures and policies, develop and implement comprehensive systems to solve organisational problems. Enjoy long-term planning and goal setting. Usually well informed, well read, enjoy expanding their knowledge and passing it on to others. Forceful in presenting their ideas.

		Key traits
INTJ	**Mastermind** most independent	They are serious, analytical and perfectionists. They have original minds and great drive for implementing their ideas and achieving their goals. Quickly see patterns in external events and develop long-range explanatory perspectives. When committed, organise a job and carry it through. Skeptical and independent, have high standards of competence and performance - for themselves and others.
ENTP	**Inventor/visionary** most inventive	Quick, ingenious, stimulating, alert, and outspoken. Resourceful in solving new and challenging problems. Adept at generating conceptual possbilities and then analysing them strategically. Good at reading other people. Great problem solvers, discoverers and re-inventors of the world. Their insights into the world around them, their ability to see new ways of putting things together and making them work can bring them great success in virtually any industry or human pursuit that interests them. They get bored by routine, will seldom do the same thing the same way, apt to turn to one new interest after another.
INTP	**Thinker** most conceptual	Seek to develop logical explanations for everything that interests them. Theoretical and abstract, interested more in ideas than in social interaction. Quiet, contained, flexible, and adaptable. Have unusual ability to focus in depth to solve problems in their area of interest. Skeptical, sometimes critical, always analytical.
ESTJ	**Guardian** most forceful	Practical, realistic, matter-of-fact. Decisive, quickly move to implement decisions. Organise projects & people to get things done, focus on getting results in the most efficient way possible. Take care of routine details. Have a clear set of logicial standards, systematically follow them and want others to also. Forceful in implementing their plans.
ISTJ	**Inspector** most reliable	Steadfast, quiet, serious, earn success by thoroughness and dependability. Practical, matter-of-fact, realistic, and responsible. Decide logically what should be done and work toward it steadily, regardless of distractions. Take pleasure in making everything orderly and organised - their work, their home, their life. Value traditions & loyalty.
ESFJ	**Provider** most harmonious	Warmhearted, conscientious, and cooperative. Want harmony in their environment, work with determination to establish it. Like to work with others to complete tasks accurately and on time. Loyal, follow through even in small matters. Notice what others need in their day-by-day lives and try to provide it. Want to be appreciated for who they are and for what they contribute. "Give and ye shall receive" is their motto.
ISFJ	**Nurturer/Conservator** most loyal	Extremely dependable, loyal, and committed. They are quiet, reserved, modest, and unassuming. ISFJ's like to be of service and they go to great lengths to be helpful. They behave as they are supposed to and don't question the established way of doing things. ISFJ's are down-to-earth, practical, conscientious and painstakingly diligent. Their mottos: "Waste not want not" and "If you want something doing right, do it yourself."

Type	Descriptor	Interaction style	Intellect	Motivation	How to influence	Default state	Temperament	Potentially - The Most	
								Positive	Negative
ESTP	Promotor	In charge	Tactics	Enjoyment	Show me the path to money	Excited	Improviser	Fun	Impulsive
ISTP	Mechanic Crafter	Chart the course	Tactics	Enjoyment	Show me the prototype	Excited	Improviser	Pragmatic	Unpredictable
ESFP	Performer	Get things going	Tactics	Enjoyment	Let me make it fun for people	Excited	Improviser	Generous	Impatient
ISFP	Composer	Behind the scenes	Tactics	Enjoyment	Give me time to see what it brings for me & others	Excited	Improviser	Artistic	Fickle sensitive

Type	Strength	Weakness	Stress	Love	Praise	Hate
ESTP	Best at adapting to change	Lowest tolerance to the routine	Mundane	The finer things in life & to improvise	Lap up any praise will probably expand on accomplishments	Monotony, conventionality & oversensitivity
ISTP	Best physical problem solvers	Distrust their own feelings and try to ignore them	Lack of independence	Adventure & to do their 'own thing'	Prefer in message they can read in private	Lack of privacy, disrespect & loss of control
ESFP	Very accepting of others	May neglect duties and responsibilities for immediate pleasure	Commitments & inflexibility	Spotlight	More flatttery the better & may feel slighted if don't get enough	Loneliness
ISFP	Gifted at creating things which will strongly affect the senses	Sensitive to criticism	Time pressure	Type most likely to believe 'love is the answer'	Slightly distrustful of the sincerity of praise. Accept if viewed as sincere friendly gesture	Rejection, falseness & people who hurt others

Type	Descriptor	Interaction style	Intellect	Motivation	How to influence	Default state	Temperament	Potentially - The Most	
								Positive	Negative
ENFJ	Giver	In charge	Diplomacy	Altruism / status	Talk to me about how it helps our team succeed	Enthusiastic	Catalyst for change	Persuasive	Needy
INFJ	Counsellor	Chart the course	Diplomacy	Altruism / status	Show me how it will make the future better	Enthusiastic	Catalyst for change	Reflective	Self righteous
ENFP	Champion	Get things going	Diplomacy	Altruism / status	You need to be glad to hear my ideas	Enthusiastic	Catalyst for change	Optimistic	Childish
INFP	Healer	Behind the scenes	Diplomacy	Altruism / status	Connect the idea (& yourself) with values	Enthusiastic	Catalyst for change	Idealistic	Whiny

Type	Strength	Weakness	Stress	Love	Praise	Hate
ENFJ	Put others needs above their own	May neglect themselves	Isolation	Giving love, support, and a good time to other people. Making things happen for others	Modest and self-effacing, respond to compliments by downplaying/deflecting to share the love	Cruelty, disunity & feeling abandoned
INFJ	Quietly forceful, original, extemely intuitive about people	Type most likely to feel cannot cope	Criticism	Self development & help others develop	Take just about any positive affirmation from others they can get. Genuine praise has a profoundly positive impact	Being misunderstood & pretentious people
ENFP	Inspiring and motivating others	See no importance in maintenance-type tasks	Procedures	Life, seeing it as a special gift, and strive to make the most out of it	Means a lot though they may downplay how much.	Inauthenticity, betrayal & boredom
INFP	Very accepting of others & defenders of human injustice/rights	Do not like to deal with hard facts & go to great lengths to avoid conflict	Decision-making	Accept others without question. Art	Take just about any positive affirmation from others they can get. Deeply appreciate others valuing their novel ideas	Stereotyping & feeling overwhelmed

Type	Descriptor	Interaction style	Intellect	Motivation	How to influence	Default state	Temperament	Potentially - The Most Positive	Potentially - The Most Negative
ENTJ	Fieldmarshall	In charge	Strategy	Pragmatism	Describe how it enhances the strategy	Calm	Theorists	Commanding	Bossy
INTJ	Mastermind	Chart the course	Strategy	Pragmatism	Draft the road map and expect my input	Calm	Theorists	Independent 2nd highest IQ	Insensitive
ENTP	Inventor	Get things going	Strategy	Pragmatism	Be open to improving the program overall	Calm	Theorists	Inventive	Egotistical
INTP	Architect	Behind the scenes	Strategy	Pragmatism	Do your research and nail the logic	Calm	Theorists	Conceptual highest IQ	Lazy

Type	Strength	Weakness	Stress	Love	Praise	Hate
ENTJ	High level of personal power and presence	Personal power can result in alienation and self-aggrandisement	Procrastination	Challenging conversations	Take compliments in stride but don't need them. Get theirs from the results	People who wont work together, laziness & ignorance
INTJ	Supreme strategists - planning every continguency	May be unaware (and sometimes uncaring) of how they come across to others	Irrational ideas / behaviour	Put everything into a rational system	Enjoy a little validation but take it with a grain of salt. V resistant to flattery	Melodramatics, being bossed & misinformation
ENTP	See new ways of putting things together	Bored by routine seldom do things same way	Deadlines	Generating possibilities & ideas	Pumps their ego like steroids	Ignorance, closed mindedness & not being listened to
INTP	Constantly generation of new theories (prove, disprove) & seeking patterns	Appear "dreamy" and distant as constantly musing over theories in their mind	No logic found	Intelligence and the ability to apply logic	Do place value on it. Ultimately rely on their own judgment and principles.	Overly serious people, being misunderstood & stupidity

Type	Descriptor	Interaction style	Intellect	Motivation	How to influence	Default state	Temperament	Potentially - The Most	
								Positive	Negative
ESTJ	Supervisor	In charge	Logistics	Stoicism / dependable	Bring the timeline and the budget	Concerned	Stabiliser	Forceful	Demanding
ISTJ	Inspector	Chart the course	Logistics	Stoicism / dependable	Plan to track progress & measure results	Concerned	Stabiliser	Reliable	Rigid
ESFJ	Provider	Get things going	Logistics	Stoicism / dependable	Appreciate our hard work and great results so far	Concerned	Stabiliser	Harmonious	Overbearing
ISFJ	Protector	Behind the scenes	Logistics	Stoicism / dependable	Say how it will affect the people I care about	Concerned	Stabiliser	Loyal	Naïve

Type	Strength	Weakness	Stress	Love	Praise	Hate
ESTJ	Clear vision of the way that things should be	May quickly dismiss input from others	Uncertainty change	Ensure everything is running systematically	Welcome signal of their competence and value to others and so take great pride verbal praise	Disorder, not being in control of their life & being ignored
ISTJ	Decide logically then work steadily to make it happen regardless of distractions	Can be overly obsessed with structure, insist everything "done by the book"	Noise & noncompliance	Facts & figures	Likely to take it with honor and pride if about work or hobbies. Awkward and embarrassed if about anything else	Lack of leadership, feeling useless & being misjudged
ESFJ	Clear vision of the way that things should be	May quickly dismiss input from others	Uncertainty change	Ensure everything is running systematically	Desire validation and social acceptance and any compliment they receive will likely be welcomed.	Disorder, not being in control of their life & being ignored
ISFJ	Seek harmony, sensitivity to people's feelings & Memory for detail & attention to detail	Can feel taken for granted & undervalued	Last-minute changes	Harmony cooperation	Modest but crave validation and appreciation from people.	Not being appreciated, jokes at their expense & insensitivity

Carl Jung said, "everything that irritates you about others, can lead you to an understanding about yourself."

Understanding that we all have innate traits that we cannot

change, that will remain with us for life, helps us to realise that it is futile to try and change these in ourselves or in another person. It is wasted effort and time, and would be hurtful and damaging, especially if done to a child or teenager (during the impressionable state of personality development).

If we can accept what we and others cannot change i.e. the essence or core of our personality, then we are free to focus our efforts on what returns the most reward; focusing on our strengths and other people's strengths.

The tables below help identify the top ten-character traits for each personality type. This knowledge helps crystallise the essence of who you are. It also helps you succinctly describe your character to a future employer, a new manager, a new colleague, a date or new friend.

Investing into what matters most and lasts longest, will always bring the greatest returns/rewards. This-is-why, I believe placing most of your effort on developing/improving your character will return the greatest rewards in your life.

This information also highlights that beliefs, values and morals are individual i.e. Subjective. Another person's beliefs, values, morals and views of the world are their personal truths so to speak. It is important to accept that everyone's belief system is different, but that it is O.K and acceptable. It is irrational and un-intelligent to think that it is O.K for you to have your own belief system but not O.K for someone else to have their own.

As soon as you judge another person's belief system to be wrong and yours to be the only right one, you have placed yourself above them and your relationship with them is destroyed.

Only equal relationships are sustainable in the long term between, two mentally healthy adults.

Type	Trait 1	Trait 2	Trait 3	Trait 4	Trait 5
ESTP - Promoter	Fun	Adaptable	Observant	Action-oriented	Tactical
ESFP - Performer	Entertaining	Generous	Fun	Excited	Adaptable
ISTP - Mechanic/Crafter	Pragmatic	Observant	Spontaneous	Independent	Adventurous
ISFP - Composer	Creative	Accepting	Sensitive	Reserved	Excited
ENTJ - Fieldmarshall	Commanding	Resolute	Innovative	Persuasive	Autonomous
ENTP - Inventor	Inventive	Inquisitive	Catalyst	Pragmatic	Theorist
INTP - Architect	Conceptual	Critical-thinking	Competent	Socially-cautious	Independent
INTJ - Mastermind	Independent	Ingenius	Resolute	Analytical	Insightful
ENFP - Champion	Gregarious	Optimistic	Catalyst	Motivational	Creative
ENFJ - Giver	Caring	Loyal	Imaginative	Team player	Enthusiastic
INFJ - Counsellor	Altruistic	Reflective	Authentic	Original	Wise
INFP - Healer	Idealistic/dreamer	Accepting	Value-oriented	Inner peace-seeker	Creative
ESTJ - Supervisor	Forceful	Dependable	Respectable	Leadership	Productive
ESFJ - Provider	Thoughtful	Conscientious	Cooperative	Organised	Loyal
ISTJ - Inspector	Reliable	Organised	Compulsive	Private	Compliant
ISFJ - Protector	Protector	Concerned	Loyal	Dependable	Diligent

Type	Trait 6	Trait 7	Trait 8	Trait 9	Trait 10
ESTP - Promoter	Excited	Creative	Tolerant	Commanding	Mentally tough
ESFP - Performer	Spontaneous	Accepting	Aesthetics-affinity	Perceptive	Pragmatic
ISTP - Mechanic/Crafter	Hands-on	Physical-problem solver	Confident	Fun	Private
ISFP - Composer	Value-oriented	Loving	Harmonious	Dedicated	Modest
ENTJ - Fieldmarshall	Frank	Pragmatic	Realist	Decisive	Strategist
ENTP - Inventor	Routine-intolerant	Limit-testing	Enthusiastic	Debating-all-angles	Challenge-loving
INTP - Architect	Absent-minded	Logical	Theorising	Honest	Individualistic
INTJ - Mastermind	Theorising	Strategist	Serious	Innovative	Perfectionist
ENFP - Champion	Harmonious	life-of-the-party	Enthusiastic-starter	Love-life	Gift-of-the-gab
ENFJ - Giver	Authentic	Leader	Inspirational	Persuasive	Unselfish
INFJ - Counsellor	Idealistic	Individualistic	Passionate	Perfectionist	Determined
INFP - Healer	Non-directive	Reserved	Novelty-lover	Defender-of-rights	Individuality
ESTJ - Supervisor	Organised	Loyal	Strategist	Principle-centric	Honest
ESFJ - Provider	Collaborative	Dependable	Compliant	Ethical	Nurturing
ISTJ - Inspector	Practical	Perfectionist	Humorous	Realist	Matter-of-fact
ISFJ - Protector	Cooperative	Organised	Planner	Compliant	Modest

A good team knows their roles and fulfils them. A great team knows their roles but also knows each other's strengths and weaknesses and intelligently adapts accordingly (to compensate and to capitalise).

When you look at the innate strengths of different personality groups and types, you start to realise the disadvantages of having a team made from the same personality group or type. Conversely, if you have a team made up of different personality groups and types it can be a far more productive team, as-long-as it is not lead by a dictatorial person and is not permitted to be dominated by one or a few people. Anything that prevents everyone in the group from making an equal contribution, is detrimental to productivity.

The table below, contains very powerful information. It informs you on how to approach each personality type differently, in order to bring them on board, with what you are trying to achieve.

This table also identifies the key contributory role that each personality type within a group or a team naturally takes. This is priceless knowledge for anyone who wants to build a high-performing team, as it enables you to identify and recruit the best mix of people and to bring out the best in each team member.

Don't even try to convince me to do something unless you.....

Interaction style	SJ Stabiliser	SP Improviser	NF Catalyst	NT Theorist
Take Charge	ESTJ *Bring the timeline & budget*	ESTP *Show the path to money*	ENFJ *Talk with me about how it helps our team succeed*	ENTJ *Describe how it advances the strategy*
Get Things Going	ESFJ *Appreciate our hard work & great results so far*	ESFP *Let me make it fun for people*	ENFP *Are glad to hear my ideas*	ENTP *Are you open to improve the program overall*
Chart the Course	ISTJ *Plan to track progress & measure results*	ISTP *Send over the prototype*	INFJ *Let me consider how it builds toward our future*	INTJ *Draft the roadmap & expect input*
Behind the Scenes	ISFJ *Say how it will affect the people I care about*	ISFP *Give me time to see what it brings*	INFP *Connect the idea (& yourself) with our values*	INTP *Do your research & nail the logic*

"Whatever thou art act well thy part" Shakespeare

CHAPTER 4: YOUR PURPOSE

"She who has a 'why' to live can bear almost any how." Friedrich Nietzsche

In other words, if you have a purpose you will generate the energy required to deal with any challenge life throws at you.

Each personality type has a hard-wired general purpose for their life. The way your brain is wired for the cognitive processes of 'Learning' and 'Decision-making' determines your primary and secondary purpose or mission.

"Life does really begin at 40. Up until then you are just doing research." Carl Jung

Through Carl Jung's wealth of experience seeing 1000s of clients throughout his life, he discovered, that it wasn't until approximately 40 years of age that a person realised and accepted their life's purpose and took full ownership and responsibility for it. Subsequently, choosing to live their life how they wanted and not how they felt significant others wanted them to live it.

Look up your personality type acronym in the four tables below to identify which are your primary and secondary cognitive processes. Then locate them in Table 1 to see what your primary and secondary life purposes are.

I found this exercise life-affirming as it really helped me gain clarity and validation for my life's purpose, which has resulted in me writing and publishing this book.

	ESFJ	ISFJ	ESTJ	ISTJ
Dominant	F(e) - Feeling (extroverted)	S(i) - Sensing (introverted)	T(e) - Thinking (extroverted)	S(i) - Sensing (introverted)
Auxiliary	S(i) - Sensing (introverted)	F(e) - Feeling (extroverted)	S(i) - Sensing (introverted)	T(e) - Thinking (extroverted)

	ESFP	ISFP	ESTP	ISTP
Dominant	S(e) - Sensing (extroverted)	F(i) - Feeling (introverted)	S(e) - Sensing (extroverted)	T(i) - Thinker (introverted)
Auxiliary	F(i)- Feeling (introverted)	S(e) - Sensing (extroverted)	T(i) - Thinker (introverted)	S(e) - Sensing (extroverted)

	ENFJ	INFJ	ENFP	INFP
Dominant	F(e) - Feeling (extroverted)	N(i) - iNtuitive (introverted)	N(e) - iNtuitive (extroverted)	F(i) - Feeling (introverted)
Auxiliary	N(i) - iNtuitive (introverted)	F(e) - Feeling (extroverted)	F(i) - Feelng (introverted)	N(e) - iNtuitive (extroverted)

	ENTJ	INTJ	ENTP	INTP
Dominant	T(e) - Thinking (extroverted)	N(i) - iNtuitive (introverted)	N(e) - iNtuitive (extroverted)	T(i) - Thinking (introverted)
Auxiliary	N(i) - iNtuitive (introverted)	T(e) - Thinking (extroverted)	T(i) - Thinking (introverted)	N(e) - iNtuitive (extroverted)

Table 1: Primary and Secondary Purpose

	Descriptor of Purpose	Learning	Decision making	Purpose
N(i)	Wisdom	Yes		I want to wonder & reflect
N(e)	Exploration	Yes		I want to explore & live a unique life
S(i)	Dependable	Yes		I want to stay on the right path & be stable
S(e)	Experiential	Yes		I want to experience & create
F(i)	Authenticity		Yes	I want to be myself & be my own guide
F(e)	Harmony		Yes	I want to help others & live in peace
T(i)	Accuracy		Yes	I want to understand & discover
T(e)	Effectiveness		Yes	I want to win & overcome

Definition of what success means for each personality type

'Adventurers' personality type group's self-image comes from how successful they feel in the following three traits: **artistic**, **adaptable** and **audacious**

ESTP: Being engaged with the immediate external world. You do not measure success in ongoing terms, but in transient moments of achievement, moments which bring you the needed feeling of having won the day. But to experience true success, you need to look within to know yourself. Enjoying the present with someone you love, going on adventures with them. Being the centre of attention.

ISTP: A life filled with physical adventure and constant action. Being permitted to take physical things apart so you can understand how they work. Regularly solving practical problems. Being physically occupied. When you finally see your place in the world and become more content with your role.

ESFP: Spending time with the people you find fun and stimulating. You are most happy when you stick out in a crowd for being entertaining. You need a lot of hands on activities in your career and your hobbies.

ISFP: Being loved unconditionally for being yourself and living in a loving and accepting environment at home & work. Of all the types, you are the most likely to believe that "Love is the answer." For the ISFP, personal success depends upon the condition of their closest relationships, their aesthetic environment and the development of their artistic creativity, their spiritual development, and how much they feel valued and accepted for their individual contributions.

'**Dreamers**' personality type group's self-image comes from how successful they feel in the following three traits: **empathic, authentic** and **kind**

ENFJ: Involvement in the process of making things happen for other people (especially loved ones); through the accomplishments and satisfactions of those you have helped to enrich the human world with greater value, and through finding that your efforts on behalf of others have fulfilled your own life as well.

INFJ: When you have used your very deep understanding of something to do a real service for another; and If you are making good progress on your self-development and your intimate relationships are healthy. You are achieving harmony in your life.

ENFP: Is being in an environment where no one is trying to control anyone (you have low tolerance for this behaviour) and where you are permitted to be true to your internal value system. Your feeling of success depends upon the availability of opportunities to grow your understanding of the world, upon feeling that your living true to your personal value system, and upon the condition of your closest relationships.

INFP: The condition of your closest relationships, the development of your creative abilities, and the continual support of humanity by serving people in need, fighting against injustice, or in some other way working to make the world a better place to be.

'**Investigators**' personality type group's self-image comes from how successful they feel in the following three traits: **ingenious**, **resolute** and **autonomous**

ENTJ: Ensuring that if there is an action which can improve an item or a situation then it ought to be taken, and you will always be found in the midst of such action, organising, planning and leading the way forward until the best result possible has been realised. This makes success for you something that can be clearly seen, a real-world result which can be measured. And whether measured in dollars, bricks, bread or just happy people, you will know the result is due to your belief that it is just plain common-sense to try and make the best of every situation and get the most out of it for the most people.

INTJ: You need an environment where clarity and conciseness are valued/respected. You will feel irritated in a culture that is purely social for the sake of being social. A pure social environment may be experienced as ingenuine. You highly value social interaction that is centred around the meaningful exchange of ideas. You value structure, order, knowledge, competence, and logic. Above all, you value your own ideas and intuitions about the world. Your feeling of success depends primarily upon your own level of understanding and accomplishment, but also depends upon the level of structure in your life, and your ability to respect the intelligence and competence of those who share your life.

ENTJ: You quickly tire of a limiting situation. For this reason, an open road toward success is an extremely important factor in your life. You are happiest in situations where you can use your intuitive powers freely and have the space in which to think upon the aspects and angles which come to you. Without fulfilling work and the freedom to use your mind most productively, you can quickly tire. You measure your success by your "aha" moments, by the sense of satisfaction which comes as you spread your newly written map before you and contemplate the new adventure, design, investigation or conquest which has now become your road ahead.

INTP: You are happiest in situations in which you can use logic regularly to uncover truths. Although you have more simple needs from interpersonal relationships than most other types, it's very important that you keep up your extraverted relationships, rather than going it alone. If you isolate yourself, you will not feel happy or successful. Your feeling of success depends upon your opportunities to exercise your active mind, your opportunities to seek and find truth, and the condition of your relationships and extraverted life.

'**Defenders**' personality type group's self-image comes from how successful they feel in the following three traits: **dependable**, **respectable** and **productive**

ISTJ: feeling of success depends upon being able to use your experience for the benefit of an institution: also, upon the level of structure and lack of chaos in your life, and in the health and welfare of your family or other social structure.

ESTJ: You feel successful if you can live your life within your defined system of principles. But your true and lasting success will come from the ability to create and sustain good and lasting principles, and thus to address all situations in your life adequately and consistently.

ISFJ: Being able to fulfil a role providing value for others and ordering your world in a way in which safety, security & happiness is balanced against a genuine respect for the aesthetic and positive qualities of life. Lastly, being appreciated for all your selfless service.

ESFJ: You thrive best when you make the decisions and organise things to suit your own way of seeing the world. Regardless of your station in life, you are at your best when it involves caring for and about others, measuring your success by the happiness and gratitude which is reflected back to you from the people in whose lives you play a part.

CHAPTER 5: THE WORLD MAKES MORE SENSE

"Your eyes are useless if your mind is blind." Anonymous

Some people feel strongly that categorising humans in any shape or form is bad. I disagree, and here's why. The process of categorising is an essential step in the process of learning and understanding. If we did not label things and categorise them, we would not be able to even acknowledge their existence or be able to talk about them, never mind accepting them as O.K.

In my opinion, it is not categorising or labelling that is bad, it is the way humans choose to use them, which is either helpful or unhelpful. If someone uses a label to unintelligently judge another person as less than themselves i.e. All people in the 'Dreamers' personality group are lazy hippies or ENTJs are all ruthless dictators. Then, it reflects their ignorance but does not mean that all categorising is unhelpful or bad.

Humans are the most intelligent and complicated mammals and therefore, their behaviours can appear entirely random at first glance. However, once personality theory is fully understood, more meaningful patterns in human behaviour appear and the world starts make more sense. It is a complete 'eye-opener.'

An important fact (the most important fact in this book), which I really hope sinks in, is that, one personality group is not better than another and there is no personality type which is better or more important than another.

The second important fact to be aware of is: 'whatever personality group or type makes up the biggest proportion of a population, it will usually be perceived as the 'norm.' This is the same principle for any trait i.e. height. If a UK adult male is approx. 5 ft 9" he is looked at as being of average height or normal: however, one inch below this height and he is viewed as short. If he is shorter that 5ft 7 he will be treated as weird and called names like 'midget.'

The ISFJ makes up the biggest personality type group within the female population (19.4%). The ISFJ personality type tends to be viewed by society as the female 'norm.' This then becomes the cultural expectation for how a woman 'should' be. Cultural pressure is then applied upon all females to comply with this 'stereotype' of what a woman should be. ESFJ makes up the second biggest personality type for females. Both ISFJs and ESFJs regularly engage in 'here & now,' functional conversation to find out how everyone is, what everyone is up to, so they can constantly compare and evaluate what is conventional. This is where the female stereotype of being verbose 'busy bodies' and 'gossipers.'

ISFJs 'protectors,' are known for always maintaining their own attractive appearance and the attractive appearance of all they are responsible for. They are very sensitive/emotional. They will not say or doing anything that hurts anyone's feeling. They attentively look after those they are responsible for. Being modest, extremely dependable, loyal, hardworking and behaving how they are supposed to.

The ISTJ makes up the biggest personality type group for males. Therefore, men are expected to be reserved, on-the-ball, unemotional, but organised and decisive (strong silent type). Therefore, if you are a man and you speak openly about your feelings, you may be viewed as not 'real' man.

The third important fact to be aware of is: overly prescriptive/rigid 'norms' or roles imposed by society, religion, communities or families upon an individual are unhealthy and can have damaging impact upon a child's psychological development.

The table below provides some very powerful knowledge (if applied intelligently), regarding the motivation, thinking, communication styles and behaviours of the four personality groups: in a clear, concise and structured way.

Personality groups	Adventurers	Defenders	Dreamers	Investigators
Preference letters	SPs	SJs	NFs	NTs
Communication type	Concrete		Abstract	
Cogntive orientation	Observant		Introspective	
Group's primary descriptor	Resourceful	Organised	Authentic	Inquiring
Implementation	Pragmatic / Betterment	Cooperative / compliant	Cooperative / compliant	Pragmatic / Betterment
Character	Artisan	Guardian	Idealist	Rational
Communication purpose	Harmony	Functional	Form a theory	Confirm a theory
Discussion style	Expressive	Current importance	Meaningful	Factual
Sharing opinion	Descriptive	Practical	Metaphoric	Hypothetical
Persuasion Style	New way is best	Current way is best	Exageration	Technical logic
Intellect	Tactical	Logistical	Diplomatic	Strategic

	Personality groups	Adventurers	Defenders	Dreamers	Investigators
Personality type	**Directive role**	**Operator**	**Administer**	**Mentor**	**Coordinator**
	Extroverted role	Promoter (ESTP)	Supervisor (ESTJ)	Teacher (ENFJ)	Fieldmarshall (ENTJ)
	Introverted role	Crafter (ISTP)	Inspector (ISTJ)	Counsellor (INFJ)	Mastermind (INTJ)
	Informative role	**Entertainer**	**Conservator**	**Advocate**	**Engineer**
	Extroverted role	Performer (ESFP)	Provider (ESFJ)	Champion (ENFP)	Inventor (ENTP)
	Introverted role	Composer (ISFP)	Protector (ISFJ)	Healer (INFP)	Architect (INTP)
	Character	Artisan	Guardian	Idealist	Rational
	Interest				
	Education	Artcraft	Commerce	Humanities	Sciences
	Preoccupation	Technique	Morality	Morale	Technology
	Vocation	Equipment	Material	Personnel	Systems
	Mode of living				
	Present	Hedonism	Stoicism	Altruism	Pragmaticism
	Future	Optimism	Pessimism	Believing	Skepticism
	Past	No real benefit	It's gone forget it	Key to hidden truths	No regrets
	Place (percepton)	Here	Gate	Path	Intersection
	Time	Now	Yesterday	Tomorrow	Intervals (measurable)

Personality groups	Adventurers	Defenders	Dreamers	Investigators
Value				
Default emotional state	Excited	Concerned	Enthusiastic	Calm
Trusting	Impulse	Authority	Intuition	Reason
Yearning	Impact	Belonging	Romance	Achievement
Seeking	Stimulation	Security	Identity	Knowledge
Prizing	Generosity	Gratitude	Recognition	Respect
Aspiring	Virtuoso Excels in technique	Executive	Sage	Wizard
Social Role				
Romance	Playmate	Helpmate	Soulmate	Mindmate
Parenting style	Liberator	Socialiser	Harmoniser	Individuator
Leading style	Negotiator	Stabiliser	Catalyst	Visionary

From the concise knowledge you have now assimilated from the above table, you will have started to realise, human behaviour makes more sense and is less random than perhaps you previously thought.

Now, answer the following questions (most of the information required to answer correctly is contained in the table above).

1. Dictatorial, dogmatic organisations i.e. this could mean your Family, religion or society are most likely to view 'Adventurers' as rebels or as a threat to their established rules and way of life (extroverted perceivers include, ESTP, ESFP ENFP & ENTP).

Why?

2. If a relationship is no longer fun, which personality group is most likely to end the relationship?

Why?

3. Which personality group is most likely to be devastated if their long-term romantic relationship ends?

Why?

4. If you are talking about how you think our lives will be like in the future, which personality group would be most interested?

Why?

5. If there is a disaster and you could pick a person to be the leader, which personality group would you want them to be from?

Why?

6. If you were going on a night out, which personality type would you most want to turn up?

Why?

7. Which personality type would you pick to organise your wedding?

Why?

8. If you were feeling depressed which personality type would you speak to?

Why?

9. If you had legal documents that needed filling in, which personality type would you ask to help you complete this task?

Why?

10. If you are at the pub and there is a quiz night. Which personality type would you want on your team?

Why?

11. Which personality type is most prone to risk-taking? (you will need to deduct the answer yourself, referring to what you have read so far in this book)

Why?

12. Which 4 personality types are most likely to cheat on their partner? (you will need to deduct the answer yourself, referring to what you have read so far in this book)

Why?

All the correct answers to these questions can be found at the back of this book.

Have you ever asked yourself why are some people so popular and well liked? What generally defines a 'good' person?

Is it because they are really the best person? Or do you think it is mainly to do with perception i.e. how we perceive each personality type?

Well, let's see if I can predict who will be viewed as the nicest person, from just looking at the four psychological preference pairs.

O.K, well let's think. Firstly, I am going to predict that this person is going to have the psychological preference letter of 'F.' Why? Well 'F' means this person prefers to make their decisions based on how they will impact other people's feelings. So, it is highly likely that they will be an 'F' as everything they do that is observable will appear to thoughtful and kind to others. They will be perceived as 'nice,' whether they are actually or not.

Secondly, I am going to predict that they have the psychological preference letter of 'P.' Why? Well 'P' generally means they are perceived to be more open and less judgemental. They are not authoritarian, so people feel relaxed and accepted.

Thirdly, combination of the 'N' and the 'F' results in the highest level of agreeableness and desire to create harmony and to put a person's morale above all else. They are the most likely to be perceived at altruistic as they are naturally motivated to help people achieve their potential without wanting anything in return (just knowing they have helped another progress is reward enough).

Lastly, they are likely to be an 'E' extrovert as they are energised by interaction with others, so communicate strongly by their high energy that they love being with you.

O.K let's test my prediction.

Yes, personality research repeatedly shows that ENFPs are the most loved of all 16 personality types. You could have predicted this yourself, just by looking at the table above.

Here's two famous examples of the personality type ENFP:
1. Will Smith
2. Sandra Bullock

Do you agree that Will Smith & Sandra Bullock are generally liked by everyone? How many people have you met that dislike them or have a bad word to say about them?

It is important to point out that how we perceive others says more about us than them. ENFPs are perceived as the nicest or the best people. However, factually speaking ENFP are not any better than any other personality type. It is in fact only a person's character that defines how mature, developed and productive they are as a human being, not their personality type.

Do you think I can predict who earns the most money on average, just by using the four psychological preference pairs?

I would say the biggest predictor of money-making is someone whose preference is to make decisions logically and not upon how the decisions will impact other people's feelings.

This means we need to pick people with the psychological preference letter 'T' for Thinkers.

I would also say 'E' for extroversion, because their energy is focussed externally (upon the world outside their mind), so they tend to be more efficient and effective at making key connections and networks of influence, which help them make more of their ideas a reality. They are also generally better at marketing themselves, their value and their accomplishments, increasing their chances of promotion over introverts.

The combination of the 'T' and the 'E' results in personality types who do not let people's feelings get in the way of them taking charge and making and implementing logical decisions. They are the personality types who are known for scoring low on agreeableness i.e. are not viewed as people-pleasers. Also, they are the personality types which people perceive as being the 'meanest.'

I also predict that they will be a 'J' judger, as their drive to structure and organise the world around them, means they are more likely to produce a realistic, robust plan and implement it effectively.

The two personality types that on average, earn the most money are:

1. ENTJ – Bill Gates
2. ESTJ – Alan Sugar (research has shown that this personality type is usually the most disliked personality type)

Once again, perception is not, I repeat not based on fact. ENTJ and ESTJ personality types are not worse or better than any other personality type. Yes, they are more likely to be hated or disliked than any other personality type, but this is a result of emotion driven perception and has no factual basis i.e. there is no intelligent, rational reasoning that underpins this prejudice.

ENTJ & ESTJ may be more likely to earn more than any other personality type, but they are not more likely to be successful than any other personality type. Remember success is subjective and can only be defined by the individual.

INTP, INTJ, INFP and INFJ, in that order (left to right) score the highest on IQ tests. But this doesn't mean they are any more 'intelligent' than any other type of personality. This means the way their brains are wired i.e. 'Strategic and diplomacy' intellects are linked to the intelligence that IQ tests favour/value (were designed to be biased towards/measure).

I will state again, it is not someone's personality type which defines how developed their character is i.e. How close they are to achieving their full potential (actualised – Google Abraham Maslow, 'Self-Actualised).

Their personality type is a given, they cannot decide to become a different personality type. However, anyone can decide to develop their character to constantly improve their self and strive to be their best self i.e. Fulfil their potential.

No personality type is better or more important than another. Fact.

Our perceptions are subjective/biased, a type of an illusion, false judgement, prejudice, not factual.

Example: the INFJ is perceived to be the most altruistic of the 16 personality types. They are viewed this way because of their brain wiring. Their innate aspiration is to become a sage for everyone. Consequently, when they get to assist someone with their wisdom and it has a life-changing impact on the recipient, the INFJ is unlikely to seek or accept physical payment.

However, the massive buzz an INFJ gets from their wisdom being sought and valued is payment enough, as it is like a drug for them. This is why INFJs have always been the shaman or the witch doctor of the tribe or community; and in more recent times the psychiatrist or therapist, because their wisdom is rarely acknowledged, appreciated or valued, so if they can attain a high status position, where their expertise is valued, they are likely to take it, no matter what the monetary reward level. They are not truly altruistic (no one is). It is being revered for their wisdom i.e. The expert status, that is an INFJ's innate motivation.

It is important to remember this, that there are no personality types that are the 'saints' (only by perception) and there are no personality types that are the 'sinners' (only by perception).

Remember there are 'horses for courses.' Personalities have evolved for a reason. When you understand that reason, you will value each personality type equally.

Let me give you a few examples:

1. If you have an important decision to make and you want to know all the facts first. Speak to an INTJ, you will not regret it. You will quickly learn to value and respect them

2. If you have a business and you want an operations manager, who will respect you as the ultimate authority, take charge, take full responsibility/accountability, be organised, efficient and effective, then recruit an ESTJ. You will quickly learn to value and respect them

3. If you are organising a works party and you are looking to pick a host. Then choose an ESFP, you will not be disappointed. They are natural entertainers and will cre-

ate the perfect 'let your hair down' atmosphere and a great night will be had by all. You will quickly learn to value and respect them

Remember, if you don't judge as fish as incompetent because they are out of water, you value and respect each personality type equally and your quality of life will be greatly enhanced by your association with each of type. Yes, variety is much more than 'the spice of life.'

In order to fully unwind you need to spend regular time with like-minded friends. However, consciously seek a friend from each personality group and your life will be enhanced and enriched. Firstly, because you will gain a 360 degree view of the world, through their diverse perspetives.

Remember, how you view other personality types informs you more about your fallible human perception process than it tells you anything factual about the other person.

Use this personality knowledge to help you accept everyone for who they are and not to excuse unfair and inaccurate judgements.

Carl Jung said (and I paraphrase), "there is no wrong or right choices, only, either poorly informed decisions that are perception based (ignorance), or the best decisions which are fact based (the first requires no thinking and the latter requires proactive thinking i.e. The gathering and analysing of all available facts, most importantly speaking to others)."

If you want to know why somebody behaves in a certain way, or want to know what someone is thinking or feeling, ask them.

CHAPTER 6: YOUR IDEAL ROMANTIC PARTNER

"We're not perfect; neither are we perfect for each other; however, we are good for each other and are committed to encouraging and helping each other fulfil our potential!"

The first point to be mindful of when searching for your ideal partner is this:

"Until you accept yourself as you are and genuinely love yourself i.e. are content living on your own, you will not have the capacity to accept someone else for who they are and be capable of achieving a 'real' love relationship.

When it comes to choosing a romantic partner, the following factors have been shown to be of instinctive priority:

1. Propinquity: we are most likely to become attracted to and form a long-term partnership with, someone we see regularly, who lives close by and who we have a close connection with i.e. your sister's friend. This is the single biggest factor.
2. Socioeconomic: we tend to be attracted to people who have a similar social status to ours i.e. similar background, education and financial position. This is partly to do with factor number 1 propinquity, as we are most

likely to be attracted to someone who goes to the same places we do. However, it is also about a perception of equal status and fitting in with our tribe so to speak i.e. our family, friends and community, to which we identify with and belong. Lastly, it is also about seeing eye to eye, having compatible outlooks and expectations.

3. Physical attractiveness: this is not solely about genetic traits, which are out of our control, the biggest factors are to do with a healthy appearance i.e. being physically fit, smelling nice, dressing well and good grooming. However, we instinctively find people that either resemble family or are opposite looking to family most attractive. Both instincts are connected to our survival instinct. We are wired to bond with our own but also to seek gene diversity.

4. Psychological familiarity: enabling you to re-create the dynamics of intimacy which feel comfortable, as they are familiar to you. Re-creating what is 'normal' for you: a reflection of your own upbringing, intimacy, parental relationships and circumstances

5. Character: confident, cheerful, friendly, kind, honest, humorous and trustworthy

6. Personality type: it appears by research that both similarity and opposites attract. We feel most comfortable with those, who think and feel in a similar way to us but are more curious and excited by those who think and feel differently to us.

You may have noticed that out of the top 6 reasons for how we choose a romantic partner, personality type comes last and it is unlikely to be a conscious part of our decision.

This is because when we fall in love it is not usually a rational decision made by the logical reasoning part of the brain, the cerebral cortex. Rather the decision is made by the limbic system in our brain. The limbic system in our brain is responsible for the experience and expression of emotion. The Limbic system does not have the ability to rationalise.

This is probably why we describe it as 'falling' in love because it just happens, and we can't explain why. It is a process outside of our conscious control. When asked why we love someone, we do not feel able to explain, until our cerebral cortex has had a chance to construct rational guesses (ascribing retrospective reasoning).

This helps to explain why so many people choose a romantic partner who is not an ideal partner. This is particularly evident in extreme cases i.e. when a person keeps choosing long term partners who treat them badly. Unfortunately, they are attracted to these bad partners at a less than conscious i.e. emotional level. These partners are meeting specific emotional needs.

In order to break these cycles of self-limiting behaviour, we need to become consciously aware of why we are behaving in this way. Then through conscious awareness we can monitor these inner subconscious desires but choose not to adhere to them. Instead we can choose to use our rational thinking (cerebral cortex) as the ultimate arbitrator, to make reasoned, better informed, more intelligent choices.

Another important factor in 'falling-in-love' is the hormone induced state called 'limerence,' which is what typically people view as 'love.'

We often enter this 'limerence' state through only one or two encounters with our 'love-interest.'

When you are in a state of limerence, your body produces heightened levels of norepinephrine, which is like adrenaline. This has the effect of increasing alertness and arousal. Also, dopamine levels are high, making you feel intense pleasure when you perceive that your love interest reciprocates in the slightest degree.

Testosterone levels increase, leading to higher risk-taking behaviours and strong desires to be physically intimate with your love interest. Increased levels of Phenylethylamine give you heightened focus, attention, goal-directed behaviour, and drive for task-completion.

Estrogen levels increase, leading to the increased likelihood of obsessive, romantic fantasizing.

Limerence is a natural drug-induced-state, that is characterized by high levels of stress, and is literally like living ina romantic thriller created by Hollywood.

Limerence, on average, lasts 2-3 years. Once limerence ends, it can feel a bit like waking up with an ugly stranger after a night of heavy drinking!

Does anyone else feel the same as me? That who we choose to have an intimate, long term relationship with i.e. Live with, is really important for our own health and wellbeing and warrants a greater investment of energy and time than: "Oh they happen to be at the right place at the right time, look O.K and have triggered a chemical reaction in my body that makes me feel addicted, impairing my ability to reason effectively. Consequently, I will live with them until the addiction ends and I will then replace them with another addiction!"

Typically, when someone's limerence state ends and an opportunity for 'real-love' presents i.e. accepting someone for who they are and supporting them to fulfil their potential, they choose to end the relationship (which feels mundane) i.e. "I have fallen out of love with you."

The main reason for ending the relationship is often that the person is now in a limerence state with someone else (you can only feel limerence/'superficial love,' for one person at a time). The new love-interest may not have any real superiority to the person you just left.

However, the human collateral damage may be colossal i.e. for the your just dumped-partner – a permanent loss of trust in intimacy, and perhaps children not being able to live with a beloved parent anymore and forming a life-time 'lack-of-trust in long term relationships.

When I hear people say trite statements like, "well, you can't help who you fall-in-love with!" I think are we talking about a toddler who filled their nappy because they have no self-control or a fully-grown human adult, supposedly the most intelligent mammal on the planet.

How can we think it is acceptable or sensible for an adult to use more intelligence when choosing which brand of coffee to buy than who to live with or marry or have children with!

Here are a few indicators that a person is in a healthy position and is ready for 'real-love:'

1. They do not employ the strategy of escaping a challenging long-term relationship through cheating. Rather they maturely work through relationship issues with their partner and then mutually agree whether their relationship has run its course. Relationships last as-long-as they are mutually beneficial i.e. both partners are bringing the best out of each other, supporting/encouraging each other's personal development.
2. They love them self and are self-fulfilled. They are not seeking a partner to give them a healthy self-esteem or make them feel valued and worthy.
3. They are not seeking happiness from intimacy. Because if they are not happy on their own, they will not be happy in an intimate partnership once the limerence fades
4. They are fully independent, physically, mentally, emo-

> tionally, financially and spiritually. They are not seeking a partner to look after them.
>
> 5. They are seeking a partner for the sole reason that they want to enhance another person's life.

The personality information I will now share with you, will help you navigate through the limerence trap and find your ideal partner, who you are more likely to develop real love with.

It is important to be aware that 'falling-in-love' means distinctly different things to each of the 16 personality types.

The table below offers a succinct insight into each personality type's preference for how they fall in love and what they mean when they say the romantic words, 'I love you.'

Type	How they like to fall in love	What I mean when I say I love you
ISFJ	Observantly, patiently and open-heartedly	I value your happiness as my own
ENFP	Intensely, excitedly and passionately	I'm enthralled by you
INFP	Grandly, deeply and romantically	Loving you has become a part of who I am
ENFJ	Passionately, considerately and deeply	I will never stop trying to make you happy
INTJ	Slowly, deliberately and secretly	I see a future with you
ENTJ	Evenly, guardedly and safely	I would do anything on earth to protect you
INTP	Cautiously, curiously and sparingly	I will never stop trying to understand you
ENTP	Curiously, quickly and obsessively	I'm fascinated by you
ISTJ	Steadily, patiently and quietly	I will maintain my commitment to you come hell or high water
ESTJ	Purposefully, deliberately and decisively	I will spend my life striving to provide for you
ISTP	Off-handedly, unintentionally and conveniently	I want to prioritise you
ESTP	Boldly, brashly and assertively	I want to be your superhero
INFJ	Slowly, guardedly and cautiously	I trust you with my heart
ESFJ	Passionately, conventionally and considerately	I want the world to know that you're on my team
ISFP	Carefully, romantically and serendipidously	We are meant for each other
ESFP	Openly, affectionately and enthusiastically	I choose you

Seeking a partner is different to seeking a group of friends who you can regularly hang out with. Research shows that the friends we tend to hang with are more likely to be from the same personality type group as us.

This is because we are drawn to people who it is easy and relaxing to be with. Ones that are easy to understand, who instantly understand us and who are not hard work, confrontational or embarrassing to be with i.e. they are people who energise you and do not sap energy from you.

However, when seeking an intimate partner, you need someone who will challenge you and demand the best from you.

As a healthy, well-adjusted adult, you are more likely to be drawn towards individuals who have strengths which you are missing. When two opposites function as a couple, they become a better-rounded, functioning unit. They are complimentary and predisposed to being more productive as a unit.

There is also the theory that your natural attraction to your opposite is a subconscious way of forcing you to deal with the weaker aspects of your own nature. Naturally, as opposites you will have significant issues to overcome, in order to accept each other as you both are. This process results in both individuals becoming more open, accepting and being able to understand themselves and each other and becoming more adept at communicating how they feel and what they want, in a respectful way. In time, as you synergize with your intimate partner, you will to a degree emulate their strengths and they yours.

Your attraction to the opposite personality is your subconscious mind driving you towards a higher chance of surviving and thriving, due to the following:

1. Natural maintenance of your self-esteem as your opposite naturally values your strengths as they are their weaknesses

2. A mutually beneficial partnership, as tasks can instinctively be divided by strengths and a balance and equality is naturally achieved

3. An introvert will be more balanced and productive as she/he is encouraged to interact with the external world more and an extrovert will become more balanced and productive as she/he is encouraged to be reflective more regularly

4. Becoming a more complete individual, by causing you to face the areas in life which are most difficult to you but return the biggest rewards

Please see the table below for guidance on your ideal romantic partner. There is a rapidly increasing body of evidence to support this 'ideal partner' theory due to the phenomenal growth of the on-line dating business, which use this theory amongst other factors like education, socioeconomic and hobbies etc. to create their love-matching algorithms. It turns out that this theory is a pretty accurate predictor for how long romantic relationships will last and the levels of happiness reported.

According to David Keirsey's research, every type's primary ideal long-term romantic partner is their complete opposite...except for the second letter, which must be the same.

However, an ever-growing body of evidence from online dating success, confirms something that is a little more complicated.

The most important factors in identifying your ideal romantic partner are:

1. The dominant cognitive function is the same preference type,
2. But it has the opposing energy focus e.g. An ISFJ's

dominant cognitive function is introverted Sensing (Si) so their ideal romantic partner's dominant cognitive function needs to be extroverted Sensing (Se).

The next most important factor is that the mode of gathering information is the same i.e. iNtuitives matched with iNtuitives and Sensors matched with Sensors.

The third factor being what David Keirsey's research evidenced, that all the rest of the preference letters are opposing i.e. ISFJ's ideal romantic partner is an ESTP

So, the age-old catchphrase 'opposites attract' is in part true.

The table below takes all the above criteria into account for you, so you can rapidly identify your primary, secondary and in some instances your third ideal romantic partner.

	Ideal Romantic Partner		
	Primary	Secondary	Third
ESFJ	ISFP	INFP	ISTP
ISFJ	ESTP	ESFP	N/A
ESTJ	ISTP	INTP	ISFP
ISTJ	ESFP	ESTP	N/A
ESFP	ISTJ	ISFJ	N/A
ISFP	ESFJ	ENFJ	ESTJ
ESTP	ISFJ	ISTJ	N/A
ISTP	ESTJ	ENTJ	ESFJ
ENFJ	INFP	ISFP	INTP
INFJ	ENTP	ENFP	N/A
ENFP	INTJ	INFJ	N/A
INFP	ENFJ	ESFJ	ENTJ
ENTJ	INTP	ISTP	N/A
INTJ	ENFP	ENTP	N/A
ENTP	INFJ	INTJ	N/A
INTP	ENTJ	ESTJ	ENFJ

Why is it important for your 'primary ideal partner's second letter to be the same as yours e.g. ESFJ and ISFP?

'Sensor (S)' and an 'iNtuitive (N)' are not communicating on the same wave-length and this makes the maintenance of a healthy, happy relationship, in the long-term 'hard work.'   Particularly when stressful life events occur, as this is when misunderstandings in communication can have a strong negative emotional impact upon the quality of your relationship.

Thus, there is the likelihood of more frequent and severe conflict due to unintended misunderstanding.

A romantic partnership between an 'S' and an 'N' is much less likely to succeed in the long term due to a 'perception' of inequality and mutual disrespect developing. This is a direct result of having opposite modes of communication. Consequently, you are less likely to see eye to eye and more likely to miss-read and miss-judge each other, which is more likely to result in emotional hurt and relationship damage.

As a sensor you are concerned with what is actual, present, current, and real. You notice facts and remember details that are important to you. You like to see the practical use of things and learn best when you see how to use what you're learning. Experience speaks to you louder than words. Your focus is on the 'here & now.'

Your mode of operation (purpose for being) is to be industrious and dutiful. You make sure the daily operations run smoothly.

In contrast, iNtuitives pay most attention to impressions or the meaning and patterns of the information they get. They would rather learn by thinking a problem through than by hands-on experience. They are interested in new things and what might be possible, so they think more about the future than the present, or the past. They like to work with symbols or abstract theories, even if they don't know how they will use them. They remember events more as an impression of what it was like than as actual-facts or details of what happened.

The iNtuitives mode of operation is a desire to understand the big picture. The detail and practicality of the mundane, daily routine is not on their radar and they are likely to challenge the norms of life, which their 'S' partners, accept as givens. 'N's may well enquire, "Why do we need to do this at all? There must be a better way!"

For you as a 'sensor' it can feel like the iNtuitive is being difficult just for the sake of it. It may appear as if they are leaving a trail of disorder and destruction that you have to clean up afterwards. "You are just creating more work for me!"

Therefore, there is a natural tendency, once the hormonal romance has gone, for you, the sensor, to instinctively build-up evidence that the iNtuitive is inattentive, inconsiderate, unhelpful, impractical, selfish, arrogant (as they talk above your head), has too lofty ideas and their 'head's in the clouds.' And what's worse, you start feeling you are unappreciated and may feel demeaned for your 'day in day out' menial focus.

On the other hand, iNtuitives feel their visionary ideas are not listened to, or valued and that their sensor partner is too set in their ways, too rigid, too superficial and short-sighted with their priority setting. Too concerned about what other people might think and too focused on the past and compliant to tradition for the sake of it.

The consequence is that both partners feel undermined, undervalued and what's worse, feel unequal.

If you're thinking, "Oh damn it!" I already have a partner which the table above states there is a 'high chance of failure!' "What do I do?"

Well the natural gravitational pull, which over time will inevitably strive to pull you both apart is not destiny. You are both intelligent human beings and if you are keenly aware of the personality-based challenges you will face together, then by consciously and proactively working together you can make your relationship work well and last.

The benefits of a successful 'S' and an 'N' partnership are obvious and powerful: think about it, a visionary partnered with a 'here and now,' action-oriented person: this can result in dreams being turned into reality very quickly.

The small table below is the key for the larger table below it.

	Ideal
G	Good
M	O.K
L	Not easy
	Challenging

	INFP	ENFP	INFJ	ENFJ	INTJ	ENTJ	INTP	ENTP	ISFP	ESFP	ISTP	ESTP	ISFJ	ESFJ	ISTJ	ESTJ
INFP	G	G	G		G		G	G								
ENFP	G	G		G		G	G	G								
INFJ	G		G	G	G	G	G									
ENFJ		G	G	G	G	G		G								
INTJ	G		G	G	G	G	G		M	M	M	M	L	L	L	L
ENTJ		G	G	G	G	G		G	M	M	M	M	M	M	M	M
INTP	G	G	G		G		G	G	M	M	M	M	L	L	L	
ENTP	G	G		G		G	G	G	M	M	M	M	L	L	L	L
ISFP					M	M	M	M	L	L	L	L	M		M	
ESFP					M	M	M	M	L	L	L	L		M		M
ISTP					M		M	M	L	L	L	L	M		M	
ESTP					M	M	M	M	L	L	L	L		M		M
ISFJ					L	M	L	L	M		M		G	G	G	G
ESFJ					L	M	L	L		M		M	G	G	G	G
ISTJ					L	M	L	L	M		M		G	G	G	G
ESTJ					L	M		L		M		M	G	G	G	G

Important reminder: if you find out that you are in a long-term partnership with someone who is categorised as 'not easy' or 'challenging, don't throw the towel in yet. Remember, any well-adjusted individuals (no matter what their personality type) can have healthy & happy long-term relationships if they are both committed to make it work.

Please refer to chapter 2 'Personality Type Traits Detail' to quickly identify your ideal partner's traits; what they love, hate; what motivates them and what love means to them.

This information will also help you to know what to put on a dating website in order to communicate to your ideal partner that you are looking specifically for them.

Also, please check back to an earlier table in this chapter, to identify how your ideal partners' fall in love and what 'I love you' means to them.

Some people, particularly the middle-aged 'SJ' Defenders like to meet people in the traditional way and would not even think about trying an online dating website service.

Here's the problem with that approach:

Let's say you're an ISFJ female at a gym hoping that an attractive man will smile at you, so you can smile back, and then hoping he will approach you with casual banter.

A local gym would seem like the perfect place for like-minded people to meet i.e. Those who put their health and appearance first. Sounds like a great choice, get fit and meet someone fit.

Your ideal type as an ISFJ is an ESTP which make up 4% of the male population: so, for every 100 men you meet, approximately 4 will be an ESTP. O.K let's say out of 20 of these men you see, you are attracted to one of them. This means out of 500 men you meet at the gym only one of them is likely to be your ideal type and be attractive. However, 70% of the attractive men will already be in relationships. Then, you've got to hope the attraction is mutual and that it leads to a date, and that you have enough in common to be compatible.

O.K you're probably getting the message. Hoping you get lucky and meet your ideal type during your everyday routine, is highly unlikely.

Heidi Priebe carried out a survey on 16th August 2016. She surveyed 1700 people to find out which personality types they were sexually attracted to. The results are very interesting.

The table below shows the results of this research. The columns of the table identify the personality type chosen as the most 'sexually attractive' due to their personality traits.

	INTJ	INFJ	ENFJ
ENFP	23%	14%	13%
	ENFPs	ENFJ	INTJ
INFP	20%	14%	10%
	INTJ	INFP	ENTP or INTP
ENFJ	15%	13%	11%
	ENFP	ENTP	INTJ
INFJ	21%	14%	11%
	INTJ	ENFP	INFJ
ENTP	20%	15%	10%
	ENFP	INTJ	ENTJ or ENTP
INTP	15%	13%	12%
	ENFP	INTP	ENTP
ENTJ	24%	15%	1%
	ENFP	ENTP or INTP	INTJ
INTJ	26%	13%	10%
ESTP	Not enough survey responses		
	ESTP	ENFP	ISFJ
ISTP	39%	17%	11%
	ENFP	ISTJ	ENFJ
ESFP	17%	12	
	INTJ	ENFP	ISFP
ISFP	23%	16%	10%
	ENFP	INTP	
ESTJ	27%	12%	11
	INFJ	ISTJ & INTP	
ISTJ	20%	16%	
	INTP		
ESFJ	12%	Equally attracted to all other types	
	ENFP	INTJ	INTP
ISFJ	19%	16%	11%

There are some interesting observations to note from this research. Firstly, it confirms the concerns I expressed earlier regarding relying on our own subconscious instincts to pick our ideal partner during our everyday routines i.e. The ideal partner for everyone can't be just ENFP!

Interestingly, the personality types ENFP and INFJ that typically score high on emotional intelligence are sexually attracted to their ideal partners. However, it is not entirely surprising that the intuitive personality types are instinctively better at choosing correctly their ideal partner (plus the INTJ, is the only type in the 'Investigator' group, who has introverted iNtuition as their dominant cognitive function).

'Sensing' types do not exhibit sexual attraction to their ideal partner types (with a small exception of ESFP picking 12% ISTJ). The 'SJ' Defenders group being the least likely to be sexually attracted to their ideal partner and showing a strong sexual preference for 'INtuitives,' who they have least long-term compatibility with.

Unsurprisingly, ENFP, the personality type, which all types are most likely to 'love,' are the type that are by far the most sexually attractive type.

Maybe not as predictable is the second most sexually attractive type being the INTJ. This is perhaps because they tend to be extremely independent, mysterious, confident and know exactly what they want.

This research confirms my hypothesis as it relates to the three parts of the human brain and their function.

The 'reptilian,' brain stem, cerebellum is known as our autopilot.

This part of the brain controls all instinctive automatic systems i.e. breathing, heart rate, flight, fight and sex. If we are at a loud night club, it will be this part of our brain that informs us of who we are sexually attracted to (using visual information only). I will refer to this as the lower brain. Mating decision based solely on the lower brain are least likely to result in you being paired with your ideal partner.

The 'mammalian,' mid-brain or limbic systems contains and governs emotions, memories, habits and emotional attachment (limerence/superficial love). I would suggest that the subjects in the above survey, making rapid response regarding who they are sexually attracted to, based on reading personality traits, are utilising mainly their limbic system. This is because as soon as they read the personality traits an auto emotional response will occur. This process is likely to occur without any rational thinking (I would propose that the reason why subjects like ENFP, INFJ & INTJ were more successful at choosing their ideal partners, is perhaps because their limbic systems algorithms are generally better). The ancient and life-time experiential wisdom that your reptilian and limbic systems have are intelligent.

However, 'reptilian' and 'mammalian' brains do not have access to 'here & now' rational thinking, so they are what we refer to in psychology as the 'subconscious' because they are essentially pre-programmed systems (they are like a computer program with clever algorithms).

The 'human brain,' or neo-cortex, is responsible for all conscious rational activity like language, abstract thought, reasoning and creativity. The 'human brain' is the only brain that is capable of rational thought (working things out by applying relevant facts). The 'human brain' is the umpire, governor or master, the mid-brain and lower brain are slave systems; doing the bulk of the heavy day to day (mundane, lower intelligence) work.

When you're doing a habitual activity, even a highly complicated task like driving you, your rational brain is free to solve
highly complex problems, as the driving is done by the autopilot
systems (mid-brain & lower brain). This-is-why sometimes you
have moments where you can't remember driving for the last 10
minutes because it's an automatic, 'subconscious' activity.

Choosing your ideal partner, will require engaging your 'human
brain' to gather all the facts produced by 100 plus years of personality theory (starting with Sigmund Freud) and related research
that has followed on since. It is highly unlikely you will make
the best decision if you only employ your slave brains to do what
should be the 'masters' job!

That's why I recommend that everyone uses reputable online
dating services that use clever algorithms to successfully match
people, which are based primarily on your ideal personality typing, then your lifestyle and your interests etc. The online dating
agencies that spend money on this will advertise the fact. A good
example of this is 'match.com.'

Think about it, your romantic partner will have more impact on
your health and wellbeing than anyone else in your life. It is well
worth paying a monthly membership fee to a reputable online
dating agency, resulting in your quality of life being positively
impacted for the next 5,10,15,20 years (maybe even the rest of
your life), than, just taking what you think is the cheap and easy
option, but costs you incalculable loss in life quality.

Those who are in a romantic relationship with their ideal partner
are reporting higher levels of happiness and longer lasting relationships.

Enough said.

CHAPTER 7: YOUR IDEAL CAREER

"A career is not just about earning an income. It is about pursuing the essence of your life." Terry Mante

You will spend more time at work than you will any other single activity in your life. That's why, if you want a meaningful life, you need to choose a meaningful career.

I would like to introduce you to the 'Career Drivers' tool, which will help you identify what you are naturally motivated by. This will help to increase your self-knowledge and help you make more informed career choices.

The day that I discovered this tool and used it, was the day my career started. I was 44 years old when this happened. Of course, the earlier you discover your career or rather your purpose in life the better. But the good news is that it's never too late and it is still as thrilling a discovery no matter what age it occurs!

These career drivers are innate motivators, which means they are a result of your brain's hard-wiring. Consequently, these career drivers are not likely to change rapidly or significantly. There will be exceptional occasions in your life when you consciously choose to override one of your innate drivers: for example, if your primary innate motivator is 'search for meaning' you may temporarily choose to switch to your main drive being 'Material possessions' due to a choice to start a family, consequently you need to purchase a house. However, as soon as you have reached the goal of buying a family home you will revert back to your main innate motivator of 'search for meaning' and you will feel a sense of relief, comfort and relaxation in doing so.

This is very powerful information as it helps you build clarity regarding what career might be most rewarding for you, but it also, and more importantly explains clearly why you are the right person for a career direction. Knowing the 'why' builds your own conviction regarding your choice and enables you to inspire confidence of the key decision makers e.g. Your line manager that you are indeed the right person for the job, so to speak. These key decision makers become your mentors and sponsors in your development journey.

Listed below are thirty-six pairs of reasons often given by people when they are asked about what they want and need from their career.

You must evaluate the importance to you of the statements within each pair and allocate three points -- no more, no less. In other words, the possible distribution of points between the two items in a pair, for example, may be as follows:

Choice	Statement A	Statement B
1	3 points	0 point
2	2 points	1 point
3	1 point	2 points
4	0 point	3 points

A score of 3 = closest to you & 0 = least like you

	Questionnaire	Record your score (0-3)
1	a. I will only be satisfied with an unusually high standard of living.	
	b. I wish to have considerable influence over other people.	
2	a. I only feel satisfied if the output from my job has real value in	
	b. I want to be an expert in the things I do.	
3	a. I want to use my creative abilities in my work.	
	b. It is especially important to me that I work with people whom I	
4	a. I will obtain particular satisfaction by being able to freely choose what I do.	
	b. I want to make quite sure that I will be financially sound.	
5	a. I enjoy feeling that people look up to me.	
	b. Not to put too fine a point on it, I want to be wealthy.	
6	a. I want substantial leadership role.	
	b. I do that which is meaningful to me, even though it may not gain tangible rewards.	
7	a. I want to feel that I have gained a hard-won expertise.	
	b. I want to create things which people associate with me alone.	
8	a. I seek deep social relationships with other people in my work.	
	b. I will get satisfaction from deciding how I spend my time.	
9	a. I will not be content unless I have ample material possessions.	
	b. I want to demonstrate to my own satisfaction that I really know my discipline.	
10	a. My work is part of my search for meaning in life.	
	b. I want the things that I produce to bear my name.	
11	a. I seek to be able to afford anything I want.	
	b. A job with a long-term security really appeals to me.	
12	a. I seek a role, which gives me substantial influence over others.	
	b. I will enjoy being a specialist in my field.	
13	a. It is important to me that my work makes a positive contribution to the wider community.	
	b. Close relationships with other people at work are important to me.	
14	a. I want my personal creativity to be extensively used.	
	b. I will prefer to be my own master.	
15	a. Close relationships with other people at work will give me special satisfaction.	
	b. I want to look ahead in my life and feel confident that I will always be okay.	

	Questionnaire	Record your score (0-3)
16	a. I want to be able to spend money easily.	
	b. I want to be genuinely innovative in my work.	
17	a. Frankly, I want to tell other people what to do.	
	b. For me, being close to others is really the important thing.	
18	a. I look upon my career as part of a search for greater meaning in	
	b. I have found that I want to take full responsibility for my own decisions.	
19	a. I will enjoy a reputation as a real specialist.	
	b. I will feel relaxed if I am in a secure career.	
20	a. I desire the trappings of wealth.	
	b. I want to get to know new people through my work.	
21	a. I like to play roles, which give me control over how others perform.	
	b. It is important that I can choose for myself the tasks that I undertake.	
22	a. I will devote myself to work if I believe that the output will be worthwhile in itself.	
	b. I will take great comfort from knowing how I will stand on my retirement day.	
23	a. Close relationships with people at work will make it difficult for me to make a career move.	
	b. Being recognized as part of the "Establishment" is important to	
24	a. I will enjoy being in charge of people and resources.	
	b. I want to create things that no one else has done before.	
25	a. At the end of the day, I do what I believe is important, not that which simply promotes my career.	
	b. I seek public recognition.	
26	a. I want to do something distinctly different.	
	b. I usually take the safe option.	
27	a. I want other people to look to me for leadership.	
	b. Social status is an important motivator for me.	
28	a. A high standard of living attracts me.	
	b. I wish to avoid being tightly controlled by a boss at work.	
29	a. I want my products to have my own name on them.	
	b. I seek formal recognition by others of my achievements.	
30	a. I prefer to be in charge.	
	b. I feel concerned when I cannot see a long way ahead in my career.	

	Questionnaire	Record your score (0-3)
31	a. I will enjoy being a person who had valuable specialist knowledge.	
	b. I will get satisfaction from not having to answer to other people.	
32	a. I dislike being a cog in a large wheel.	
	b. It will give me satisfaction to have a high-status job.	
33	a. I am prepared to do most things for material reward.	
	b. I see work as a means of enriching my personal development.	
34	a. I want to have a prestigious position in my organization for which I work.	
	b. A secure future attracts me every time.	
35	a. When I have congenial social relationships nothing else really matters.	
	b. Being able to make an expert contribution will give me particular satisfaction.	
36	a. I will enjoy the status symbols, which come with senior positions.	
	b. I aspire to achieve a high level of specialist competence.	

Which of the 9 Career Drivers does each Statement relate to					
(which 36 question's score is to be assigned to which career driver - key for score table)					
1	Material rewards	13	Search for meaning	25	Search for meaning
	Power		Relationships		Status
2	Search for meaning	14	Creativity	26	Creativity
	Expert		Autonomy		Security
3	Creativity	15	Relationships	27	Power
	Relationships		Security		Status
4	Autonomy	16	Material rewards	28	Material rewards
	Security		Creativity		Autonomy
5	Status	17	Power	29	Creativity
	Material rewards		Relationships		Status
6	Power	18	Search for meaning	30	Power
	Search for meaning		Autonomy		Security
7	Expert	19	Expert	31	Expert
	Creativity		Security		Autonomy
8	Relationships	20	Material rewards	32	Autonomy
	Autonomy		Relationships		Status
9	Material rewards	21	Power	33	Material rewards
	Expert		Autonomy		Search for meaning
10	Search for meaning	22	Search for meaning	34	Status
	Creativity		Security		Security
11	Material rewards	23	Relationships	35	Relationships
	Security		Status		Expert
12	Power	24	Power	36	Status
	Expert		Creativity		Expert

Please add up your 9 career drivers' scores and complete the score table below.

9 Career Drivers	
Expertise	
Autonomy	
Status	
Power	
Creativity	
Material rewards	
Afilliation	
Security	
Search for meaning	

Below are the definitions of each career driver:

Expertise
Expertise relates to specialist knowledge, skills, competencies and capacity to perform unusual, difficult or specialised activities. A person with a high career driver score for expertise works hard continuously to gain additional knowledge and maintain his capability in his specialized discipline. He dislikes being out of his specialized area and is satisfied being valued as an expert.

Autonomy
This relates to being able to take personal responsibility and make personal decisions. A person with a high score for this career driver will act to increase the amount of control she has over his working life. She will tend to resist any restriction or constraint on her activities and decisions. She does not like to be directed by others and prefers to work alone or lead a small team.

Status
This relates to a need for recognition, admiration and respect by others. Status is demonstrated by symbols, formal recognition and acceptance into privileged groups. A person with a high career driver score in status aims at being highly regarded by others as well as wanting the esteem of others. She values being acknowledged and recognized as an authority in an area. For example, she wants a position of power and authority for the sake of the prestige of the position rather than the associated exercise of control.

Power/Influence
This relates to the need for dominance and having others to behave in subordinate roles. In addition, a person with a high power/influence as a career driver wants to be in charge of matters affecting policies or resource allocation.

Creativity
This relates to innovative ideas such as originating something new that bears the name of the initiator. A person with a career driver score that is high in creativity is interested in doing things that are different from what others are doing. She derives great satisfaction from creating something new and she handles failures or setbacks very well.

Material rewards
These are defined as tangible assets and include cash and other material possessions. The individual is primarily concerned with riches, and will not be affected by the unsatisfying tasks in the job. For example, such a person will change job only for material advantages regardless of how disagreeable the job tasks are.

Affiliation
This is defined as enjoying bonds of friendship, being close to others and being enriched by human relationships. A person with a career driver that is high in affiliation will initiate and develop long lasting and fulfilling relationships with others. She is committed to people and not to job task, position or organizational goals. She will continue in an unsatisfactory or unfulfilling job because of the quality of her relationship with others.

Security
This relates to the desire to know the future as well as the avoidance of exposure to unpredictable risks. She is concerned with predictability rather than a high income. She will seek an employer who has a record of stability and good employee welfare.

> **Search for meaning**
> This relates to doing things that are perceived to be valuable for their sake. A person who has a high score in this career driver is motivated to do things that are deemed to contribute to something bigger, finer or greater than himself. An example is that he will help another person rather than himself. Such a person is concerned with personal fulfilment.

We are intelligent and can adapt to most situations. Therefore, I can safely say, most people can do most jobs.

However, if we want a fulfilling career, it is unlikely to just fall into your lap.

A global poll carried out in 2019, by Gallup, found that of the world's one billion full-time workers, only 15% are engaged at work. This means 85% of employees are to a degree dissatisfied at work.

This is not as surprising as you might first think. Ask yourself honestly why you are doing the job you are doing.

Most people when asked this question express varying factors and events that lead them to their job.

Unfortunately, the reasons they provide do not tend to be under-pinned by logical thinking i.e. I am naturally good at this or I really enjoy doing this: therefore, I chose this career because it was the best match with my innate talents and passions.

If we look at the factor of personality, there are jobs that are ideal matches, jobs that are O.K matches, but there are jobs that are poor matches.

The jobs that are poor matches will be the source of high stress and low levels of satisfaction. They tend to remain a job and not a career.

They will rob you of your enthusiasm for life and result in an imbalance that will adversely affect your health and well-being inside and outside of work.

You spend most of your life at work. If you want your life to feel meaningful, then your work needs to be meaningful.

As a 'rule of thumb' for whether you are in the right 'ball-park' when it comes to a career:
firstly check which personality group you are in. Why?

1. The 'SJ's Defenders group's broad role is to keep the wheels of human industry/commerce turning' i.e. To provide and protect - Plan-Do-Check-Act. Evolution has designed the SJ's to be like 'self-sufficient' company, capable of efficiently & effectively, producing all the goods required by the human species.

They have the following transferrable traits; respect for authority, hard working, reliable, cooperative and stoic.   These are the most important traits for success in most jobs.

They ensure all the jobs required to keep the human family alive are resourced and completed; according to the agreed processes and as efficiently and smoothly as possible.

This is why evolution has ensured that this group accounts for the biggest percentage of the human race i.e. 45%, the doers, the supervisors and the managers of commerce.

The three other groups have evolved to be specialist back-up support and service functions to the human race ', to keep them healthy, happy, motivated and bestprepared for surviving the future .

2. The 'SP's Adventurers are primarily responsible to provide leisure and entertainment service to the rest of the human race.

They are risk-takers, driven to make the most of 'the moment:' wired to constantly seek out new sensory experiences.

Naturally, they show us how to make our lives fun. The benefits of been fully engaged in the present moment.

Making toys for our leisure; creating art, music, theatre, outdoor sports/pursuits, and providing the promotion of all these sources of physical leisure & outdoor adventure. Thus, improving the morale and quality of life for all. They account for 25% of human race.

3. The 'NF's Dreamers are responsible for keeping all of the human race healthy in body, mind and spirit. They have the innate desire to understand the human predicament in a holistic and deep manner. Consequently, they not only provide a healing service for all injured during their line-of-duty, but they strive to create a preventative service that reduces the chance of any future injury. They are future focussed and encourage all to do now, that, which will ensure the best future.
They account for 20% of the human race.

4. The 'NT's Investigators are the industrial analysts/inventors. Their ability to logically analyse, to predict future limitations, restraints and challenges, makes them best placed to prevent and resolve breakdowns.

Breakdowns that cannot be resolved using current methods or standard thinking.

They provide an indepth logical analysis of the problems, getting down to the root cause.

Their solutions are likely to result in novel or original ideas being generated, which may completely change the way industry produces in the future i.e. the industrial revolution, home comput-

ing, electric cars and mobile phones etc.
They account for 10% of the human race.

Please use the above personality group knowledge as a general lens, as you look at the 'Top 5 Careers' table.

You will then begin to get a rough idea regarding what career is a best-fit for you.

I think it is important to point out, that out of all the types, the ones who will probably experience mental health risk from working in an ill-fitting career are:

INFP
INFJ

INF's tend to be sensitive, creative visionaries; lovers of freedom; who are consequently the most reflective and may be viewed by their boss as absent-minded and difficult to manage.

Nature has highly specialised them to help others 'heal and grow.' But in mainstream employment, may be prone to being viewed as not 'focussed,' 'too slow,' forgetful, disorganised and 'lazy.' This experience may have an adverse impact upon their self-esteem.

This demonstrates why the principle of 'horses for course' is so fundamentally important. They more people pursue their innate strengths and passions through their career choice (even if that means creating a new original career just for you), the more likely you are to feel fully engaged and fulfilled; plus the greater the benefit to world.

The careers in the following tables provide you with examples of potential best fits. Guiding you towards the types of careers that you are more likely to enjoy and thrive in.

	Key traits	Top 5 - Best Fit Careers				
		1	2	3	4	5
ESTP	Focussed on immediate results; risk takers; creative hands-on problem solvers. Adventurous explorers	Marketing or entrepeneur	Actor	Detective	Stockbroker	Journalist
ISTP	Technical drive to understand how things physically work, data-driven problem solvers, hands on. Risk-takers. Prefer unpredictable work. Fearless, adrenaline lovers. Need challenge	Technical fields i.e. formula 1 racing mechanic, Elevator mechanic / engineer	Trouble shooter in the tech industry	Astronaut	Toy designer	Skilled trade Craftsperson
ESFP	Love to be the centre of attention and make people smile Fun loving	Entertainer	Events or recreation coordinator	Corporate Trainer or Teacher	Public relations	Adventure blogger
ISFP	Need freedom for their artistic expression and the achievement of their value oriented goals May prefer freelance work	Artist	Musician	Composer	Designer	Landscape architect
ENFJ	Help others develop. Strong desire for personal development , creative expression & further humanitarian causes	Teacher	Public relations manager	Social worker	Marriage & family therapist	Child care centre director
INFJ	Most empathic. Strong discernment of human behaviour. Best one on one Require for high autonomy - may prefer self-employment, freelance	Psychologist or therapist	Religious or spiritual careers	Author	Design or Art	Social worker
ENFP	People-centered creators with a focus on possibilities. Contagious enthusiasm for new ideas, people and activities. Empowering others - informal & flexible careers. Explorers.	Fundraiser	Personel manager	Human resource specialist	Director of education	Reporter
INFP	Need to be allowed to express their individuality in the way they work, and take advantage of their ability to see unique solutions. Explorers. High need for freedom - may prefer freelance	Mediator or alternative holistic therapist	Writer, journalist	Audio visual specialist, broadcast technician or film editor	Arts i.e. Multi media artist	Activist
ENTJ	Natural leaders. See challenges to be surmounted; they want full responsibility for surmounting them	Corporate director / leadership	Politician	Management consultant / Project management	Lawyer barrister Judge	Chief engineer

Remember, no matter how strongly you are pulled towards a career. The principle of 'try before you buy' still applies. Participate in voluntary job shadowing or work experience, to increase your understanding and relevant preparation for your preferred career choice.

	Key traits	Top 5 - Best Fit Careers				
		1	2	3	4	5
INTJ	Excel in analysis of complicated data. Best at creating and implementing innovative solutions to complex analytical problems (insatiable thirst for knowledge)	Technical careers i.e. Idustrial engineer	Science	Accountancy or legal	Computer programmer	Surgeon
ENTP	Entrepreneurial approach with least restrictions on their ingenuity. Value power, want to maximise their influence. Explorers. May prefer to set their own business up - make their own way	Inventor	Stockbroker	Lawyer	Research and development	Film producer
INTP	They have unconventional thought patterns which allows them to analyze ideas in new ways. Explorers.	Computer programmer / coder	Scientist	Architect	Information security analyst	Forensic medical examiner
ESTJ	Dedicated, direct and loyal. Excel at organising—people, projects, and operations. Like to be in control and often seek out management positions	CEO	Judge	Hotel manager	Doctor	Military officer
ISTJ	Very hard workers, dependable & meticulous. Good with facts & figures. They prefer to work alone	Business analyst	Auditor	Accountant	Services - police, military	Surveyor
ESFJ	Need to put their interpersonal skills to work to organise people and processes. Like to help people in practical, observable ways	Training facilitator	Nurse	Office manager	Event or project manager	Carer
ISFJ	Enjoy work that requires careful attention to detail and adherence to established procedures. Like to be efficient and structured in completion of tasks. Tend to have a good eye for what is aesthetically pleasing	Administrator	Healthcare	Education	Interior designer	Bookkeeper

The best fit for the military and police, which are most likely to achieve officer / manager level are ESTJ, ISTJ and ISTP, in that order. The challenge for the ISTP is accepting the trade off; compliance to authority, in order to benefit in the longterm through career success.

The types most naturally adept to the 'caring' professions are ESFJs, ISFJs, ENFJs and ENFPs.

	Reasons	Worst Fit Career		
		1	2	3
ESTP	Tasks that require being comfortable with deep emotions being regularly shared. Highly solitary and repetitive tasks or work that requires too much focus on the theoretical	Counsellor	Accountant	Accademic
ISTP	Any job that's not hands on, or doesn't require complex data-driven problem solving or requires too much social interaction or repetitive tasks	Restaurant manager	Author	Bookkeeping
ESFP	All careers where you do not have the freedom to socialise or gain public recognition. Where you have to follow rigid procedures and analyse a lot of routine data and perform a lot of mundane tasks. Need a high amount of spontaneity	Accountant	Production line operator	Administration
ISFP	A job where there is zero opportunity for creativity or self expression and lots of rules and regulations and too much social interaction	Traffic warden	Engineering	Sales
ENFJ	Naturally drawn to people person work, not systems and processes. Idealistic, seeing the best in people best avoid dealing with the darkside of human-nature. Need high amount of interaction with people	Computer programming	Criminal psychologist	Farmer
INFJ	Anything which requires 1. High amount of disturbance of their reflective thought process or 2. Regularly dealing with insignificant/trivial problems or 3. Being ingenuine or receiving criticism. Anything that requires a thinking-on-your-feet approach	Logistics manager	Customer service	Politician
ENFP	Jobs that require precision, attention-to- detail, repetition: plus rigid, structured processes, will result in significant frustration & dissatisfaction	Scientist/lab technician	Aviation engineer	Financial adviser
INFP	Jobs that encourage: 1. Direct competition with colleagues 2. Frequent conflict 3. Financial targets or that has 4. Strict rules & a lot bureaucracy or 5. Repetitve routine	Sales	Military	Law
ENTJ	If no strategic thinking is involved or if there are no significant challenges or no scope for how to deliver a project then research for a new job will be instigated	Truck driver	Production line operator	Data entry

		Worst Fit Career		
INTJ	Where a strong social element and trivial conversations are required to build rapport. Collaboration needed with a large and varied team of people. Where structured and measurable results are not possible. Having to work with people who you view as non-experts or incompetent	Sales	Hospital jobs	Social worker
ENTP	Any job with strict, rigid, regimented and mundane tasks that require high attention to detail and little or no innovation, flexibility or freedom to do things your own way. Need to work with others you view as intellectual equals	Data entry	Receptionist	Teaching
INTP	Environments where their creativity is stifled and you are micro managed. Job needs to involve a high level critical thinking	Retail	Nursery worker or child care jobs	Military
ESTJ	Where there's a lack of stability & where there's a lack of regular contact with people. Also, jobs where your exposed to frequent change & spontaneous decisions	Abstract artist	Freelance playwriter	Peschool or primary teacher
ISTJ	Don't like surprises or unpredictable environments: highly abstract work. Situations where clients can keep changing their minds & surroundings are constantly changing. Frequently dealing with theories, thoughts or feelings	Community art worker	Working with children	Psychologist
ESFJ	Jobs that do not have set hours and clear schedules that make work life balance difficult. Environments where there's pressure to sell things to people that they do not need. Solitary roles where you are unlikely to feel appreciated	Tour manager	Marketing	Software developer
ISFJ	Unpredictable work, as prefer routine and structure. Would feel uncomfortable if had to drop all other responsbilities because work duty called at any time without warning. Where constantly forced into the frontline without a plan or preparation, as prefer to work in the background without craving attention and recognition	Journalism	Estate agent	Paramedic

It is important, to not only look at what's involved in a job but also at the ethos, culture and environment of the company / organisation.

Certain cultures or environments can cause a great deal of stress for you and may be best avoided.

Be aware that good companies can be quite advanced in accommodating diversity. Therefore, despite their environment looking undesirable, they may be willing to adjust and flex their ways of working to fit you better.

There is a realisation in progressive companies that this type of flexibility results in higher engagement and better quality output.

Take a look at the following tables to identify your innate stressors.

Will become Stressed by	
Extraversion (E)	Spending too much time alone
	Not enough external stimulation
Intraversion (I)	Spending too much time with others
	Too many external distractions
Sensing (S)	Ambiguity, no clear plan or direction
	Ideas without any foundation or purpose
INtuition (N)	Having to follow exact instructions
	People who want the detail
Feeling (F)	Not having their values respected
	Conflict and lack of harmony
Thinking (T)	Illogical, subjective and hence unfair decisions
	Being forced to worry about people rather than the task
Judging (J)	Disorganised people or organisations
	Last-minute rushes
Perceiving (P)	Inflexible people or organisations
	Making decisions before they need to

	Stressful Work Place				
	1	2	3	4	5
ESTP	Rigidly enforced rules	Commitments: Having to plan too far into the future	Isolation	Quick decisions: forced to make decisions or eliminate options before they're ready	Non-challenging: mondane, repetitive routine work
ISTP	Lack of independence	Inefficiency	Controlling relationship - tight restrictions/rules & rigid structured organisations	Small talk. Dismissing my practical reality or analysis of a problem	Non-challenging: mondane, repetitive routine work
ESFP	Unable to change commitments	Analysis paralysis Data Boredom	Environment of conflict and criticism	Forcing a decision	Detailed plans Long term planning
ISFP	Constant time pressure	Lack of understanding: environment that neglects your deeply held values	Too many demands and obligations	Frequent conflict situations where others disagree or disapprove of your ideas, values or behaviour	Disregarding your practical realities
ENFJ	Highly confrontational/tense relationships environment	Receiving little or no appreciation and being subject to excessive criticism (not being understood or trusted)	Dealing with the minutia without having a clear vision of why it needs doing	Over-empathising with others to the point of losing track of your own needs	Shortsightedness
INFJ	Criticism and not being accepted, trusted and valued. Diversity not valued.	No time for future vision or support to make future vision reality	Too loud and disruptive environment: can't get enough alone time to think and reflect	Not enough self development or support of others' development	Working with a lot of negative people
ENFP	Organisation at the expense of creativity i.e death by spreadsheet	Rigid rules and procedures over relationships. Mundane, endless detail	Thoughtlessness and rudeness. Not putting people's feelings and liberties first	Not being able to use your intuition. Constraints on brainstorming, envisioning or enthusiasm	Being micromanaged: forced to make decisions before ready or make long term plans
INFP	Where your & other people's values are violated i.e employees are mistreated and freedom of expression is not valued	Too prescriptive and rigid environments that stifle your freedom and creativity	Environments where there is open conflict and disrespect. Lacking harmony	Mundane tasks, where freedom is restricted and you are being monitored and pressured to work quicker	Too much small talk and a distinct lack of authenticity
ENTJ	Procrastination: not being able to make your goals come to fruition.	Environment that lacks vision or ideas for the future	Competence being challenged	Having to be the follower instead of the leader	Dismissing your logical decisions
INTJ	Where complicated, systematic analysis of information is not required or valued	Working with people you view as incompetent, lazy or ignorant	Competence being challenged i.e. Your knowledge and advice not being respected	Being frequently required to talk about your feelings	Procrastination and lack of initiative or independency

Stressful Work Place				
1	**2**	**3**	**4**	**5**
ESTJ Lack of control (constant unexpected change, uncertainty & disruption)	Indecision or irrational, incompetent, disorganised & lazy people	Being challenged on your bottom-line approach (your focus on monetary - profit margin)	Guilt from being critical of others	Their established rules and regulations being disregarded
ISTJ Noisy or messy, disordered environment	Being rushed / unrealistic deadlines	Being told to do something illogical, without a clear plan or direction. Frequently required to be spontaneous	Frequent change	Emotionally charged situations
ESFJ Isolation Need to achieve as part of a team and feel they are helping and supporting each team member. Ensuring all are included.	Uncertainty Unstructured & disorganised environments	Dismissing how you feel Inadequate time to complete work to their own standards	Lack of emotional support	Disrupting harmony
ISFJ Noisy, messy and disordered environment. Last minute changes. Irresponsible, disorganised, procrastinating & lazy people	Overexerting yourself through saying 'Yes' too many times	Conflict or criticism. Environments filled with tension	Constantly acting as the responsible one	Lack of positive feedback (being unappreciated)

On the next page you will see a bar chart, which shows the average earnings in America for each personality type.

It is important to remember, your personality type may be a factor in how much you earn, but a lot larger determiner for how much you earn will be your level of education and the character traits of resilence, resourcefulness, drive and determination.

When I say education, I refer to formal and informal.

For example, your education regarding your self-knowledge is a key factor in earnings. Think about it, innate passion will elevate your service's unique value and therefore increase the demand for you and your unique services.

Look at myself for example, when you read this book, my innate passion lifts off the pages. I am doing what I was born to do and it shows in the unique service I am offering.

In the long term, the chances are, that I will earn more money from writing psychological self-help books and consulting/ coaching, than from anything else that I do (which I am not so good at and do not feel as fulfilled doing).

As you can see from the chart above, the personality types who are innately driven towards the entertainment, art and health-care careers (unsurprisingly tend to earn the least i.e. INFJ, ISFP & INFP)

Interestingly, the personality type who on average scores higher on IQ tests than any other personality type, the INTP, also features in the lower end of earnings. Evidencing that IQ is not the best indicator for earnings.

Not surprisingly, the ISFJ who naturally tends to overextend (take on too much responsibility, without demanding a fair reward) i.e. Likely to be modest and timid about their contribution, is less likely to be promoted than other types and as a consequence tend to earn less.

Lastly, the ISTP has a strong hands-on, technical flare, but struggles with red tape and is consequently less likely to want promoting to less-hands on and more bureaucratic work.

Remember, success cannot be determined solely by earnings; but rather by peace of mind, that comes from knowing you are fulfilling your individual purpose and potential.

Most people reading this book, will not be working in their ideal career yet. And, leaving your current job today may not be prudent or practical. In order to minimise the energy draining impact of your current job, there are certain things you can do.

Firstly, sit down and think about how you can mold your job to fit you better. For example: if you are an extrovert and you are currently sitting alone all day, is there a way you can relocate to sit with others.

Explain to your manager the disconnect between your innate personality requirements and your current job situation and how it makes you feel. Then proactively share with her your proposed plan to improve your situation, by small adjustments, which will significantly increase your happiness at work. Be explicit with your manager, so they know that the purpose of the conversation is to gain alignment and suport from her.

As long as you have a realistic plan with incremental steps for how you are going to steadily move from where you are now to your ideal career, everything will instantly feel more bearable.

But each day you must do something, no matter how tiny, that takes you closer to your ideal career. As, if you do this, I promise you, your stress levels will drop and your positive energy and levels of satisfaction will grow.

This is because you have metaphorically speaking, turned a light on at the end of the tunnel, which permits you to measure your daily progress.

CHAPTER 8: ENLIGHTENED PARENTING

"The way we talk to our children becomes their inner voice." Peggy O' Mara

Now-a-days, it seems qualifications are required for everything. Except, for the single most important job in the world, that of a parent: anyone can do that without any training whatsoever!

In my humble opinion, the best thing you can do for your children is to strive to resolve as much of your own big hang ups and issues as possible: so, you do not pass this emotional damage on to them.

Sigmund Freud was the first psychiatrist to introduce the theory of the stages of psychological development in children. He believed successfully passing through these developmental stages formed a healthy subconscious and personality.

Freud believed events in our childhood had significant influence on our adult lives and formed our personality. However, because this influence is subconscious i.e. Outside of our conscious awareness, it is almost impossible for us to resolve these issues by ourselves.

Freud believed that if we did not pass healthily through one or more of these psychological development stages during our childhood, that we were essentially stuck in that stage as adults, unable to know the origin of the issue and unable to resolve our issues and progress.

Freud developed therapeutic tools to help make our subconscious issues conscious so the issues could be logically resolved through psychoanalysis, enhanced by hypnotherapeutic techniques. These tools are called psychoanalysis.

Erik Erikson, a psychoanalyst, further expanded Freud's psychological childhood development stages theory, to include more stages that spanned a person's entire life and were more focussed on the elements of healthy socialisation.

Stage	Age	Psychosocial Issue	Relational Focus	Central Question	Associate Virtue
1. Infancy	0-1	Trust vs Mistrust	Primary caregiver(s)	Secure	Hope: Trust & Optimism
2. Early Childhood	2-3	Autonomy vs Doubt	Primary caregiver(s)	Independent	Will: Self-control & Discipline
3. Childhood (play)	4-6	Initiative vs Guilt	Family	Influential (personal power)	Purpose & direction: Self-motivated
4. Childhood (school)	7-12	Industry vs Inferiority	School	Quality Productivity	Competence: Excellence
5. Adolescence	13-19	Identity vs Role confusion	Peer group	Integrated	Healthy self identity: Feel unique and ordinary
6. Young Adulthood	20-35	Intimacy vs Isolation	Intimate Partners	Love	Mutuality (Coorporation): Healthy intimate partnerships / friendships
7. Adulthood	36-55	Generativity vs Stagnation	Mature Partnerships	Service (real love)	Real self (collaboration): building a unique legacy
8. Maturity	56+	Integrity vs Despair	Humankind	Receive service	Wisdom: fulfiled, giving back - mentor

To be clear, if you are struggling with issues related to the 'Central Question' column in the above table of the 8-stages of psychosocial development i.e. You suffer acutely from one or more of the following and it prevents you from living a fulfilled, healthy and progressive life:

Insecurity

Dependency

Can't calmly explain your point of view & listen and accept other points of view as equally valid as your own

Do not feel like a fully integrated member of society

Feel unlovable

Do not feel you have the capacity to love another

Do not believe you can provide a valuable service to others

I would recommend you seek professional psychoanalytical therapy / hypnotherapy to help you become 'unstuck' and pass through each of these eight Erikson stages. You can then live a full and rewarding life and avoid passing on any of these issues to your children. Please find therapeutic contact details at the back of this book.

I used to suffer from 'general anxiety disorder.' When I awoke in the morning every day, I would get the same sick feeling in my chest. Facing the world and trying to make an honest living, felt like I was jumping out of an aeroplane without a parachute. I would regularly have random panic attacks for no logical reason (that I was consciously aware of).

I went for a total of eight psychoanalytical hypnotherapy sessions and this anxiety disorder left me completely. No more panic attacks or sick feelings inside. Over the past 3 years, my anxiety disorder has returned twice, each time I have returned for a top-up hypnotherapy session and the feeling has once again disappeared.

My issues were related to childhood events involving my relationship with my father. As a child I believe I formed a 'man' archetype of someone I didn't feel I wanted to become or could become. I also associated 'man' with provider. Therefore, at a subconscious level, when it came to work, I never felt like I was a real man, who could compete equally with other men to earn a living. I felt like a scared child who wasn't tough enough to cope.

Looking at the Erickson stages, it would be stage 3 'childhood play' (4 to 6-year-old) that I did not pass through healthily. I identified myself as male but not fitting my infantile definition of a man. As a young child I only had my father to define men by, and I knew I was too sensitive to qualify under that narrow definition. Therefore, I suffered from an underlying feeling of guilt (not feeling good enough), lacking confidence / self-belief, influence and power. This 'general anxiety' spanned my childhood, teenage and adult life, until I was 48 years old and completed my psychoanalytical hypnotherapy sessions.

Psychoanalytical hypnotherapy places you in a relaxed and more open / receptive state, where the hypnotherapist uses Freudian techniques, such as 'free-association' to pin point the underlying root cause (developmental stage issue), and then uses guided imagery techniques to help your rational mind communicate directly to your subconscious mind and re-write your infantile & irrational programming (false beliefs).

The subconscious language is imagery loaded with emotion. The great thing is, that once your rational brain (cerebral cortex) accesses a communication path to your irrational subconscious (mid-brain/limbic system – that contains emotionally charged illogical beliefs, which haven't changed since you were a young child), the change is almost instantaneous once you enter your sleep state (that first night after your hypnosis session, your limbic system's programming is re-configured/re-programmed).

O.K so now we've covered step 1, of the good parenting guide.

Step 1: Try not to pass on your emotional damage issues onto your children

We are now moving onto step 2.

Step 2: Try not to pass on your false beliefs to your children

Morris Massey, the sociologist, believed that approximately 90% of our core personal beliefs and values are set by the age of 10 years.

The two early developmental stages where most of our self-identity and core beliefs (beliefs about our self and our world) were formed are described below:

1. **Imprinting stage (0-7):** we were like a sponge, absorbing everything around us. Accepting & generalising what we saw i.e. if dad is good 'men are good.' Accepting what we were told as true i.e. you are good, bad, stupid, clever, particularly information provided by your primary care giver(s). Establishing our core beliefs and identity

2. **Modelling stage (8-12):** we were taking more control of our learning, acting out our core beliefs. Comparing and copying people, often our parents, but also others we valued and respected. We were trying things on like different clothes, to see how we felt in them. We were impressed by specific authority figures who we attached to e.g. teachers we liked etc....

Morris Massey believed once we entered adulthood our core beliefs and values were locked in and only through the occurrence of significant emotional events (personal crisis) could core self-limiting beliefs and values be changed. Personal crisis is a catalyst for change, because we are confronted with the limitations of our subconscious false belief programming.

Imagine if a short child was constantly taught by their primary caregiver(s), that it was not O.K to be short, that short people were unacceptable, that they were inherently bad. As an adult, it is likely that they will have a core belief that they are not good enough. Consequently, would suffer from self-esteem issues.

As an adult they may well avoid dating short people as they view them as 'bad.' Consequently, they may well marry a tall person. Years later, let's say, their tall spouse cheats on them and divorces them. This personal crisis or 'Significant Emotional Event' may well be strong enough to challenge and overturn their subconscious false belief, that short people are bad and tall people are good.

The above example might sound a bit silly and unrealistic to you but believe me it is not. However, now imagine another scenario that follows the same principles but will hopefully be more relatable for you.

You are an INTJ child with ESFJ parents. Their style of parenting means they believe in socialising you into a 'highly social, agreeable, practical, productive and compliant' citizen.

You also live in America where the 'culture' is an extroverted one i.e. extroversion is viewed as 'good,' healthy and required for success.

Then, add to this situation, that as an INTJ your brain is wired to respect authority and you have a strong desire to comply with authority i.e. your parents and society.

At home your parents are stressing because they are embarrassed by you. Appearances are very important to them, as is fitting in.

They had the perfect life, career, house and car, before you came along. Now they have this alien child that appears to be a complete nerd and social misfit. They are constantly stressed around you. They are really frustrated and angry because you want to read rather than play with the kids in the streets. You state facts to other children, and they go running to their parents saying you hurt their feelings.

At parents evening at school, your teacher is telling your parents how concerned she is because you often play on your own and that you are a loner, socially awkward, not participating in group activities effectively and your parents are agreeing with her.

The parents and teacher have labelled your psychological preferences of introversion and thinking i.e. The 'drive to introspectively assimilate and share facts,' as 'bad and not acceptable.'

Your parents believe in the prevalent American culture, that you need to be extraverted to be successful, both socially and in your career. They are genuinely concerned that you have some sort of disability. They take you to the doctors, hoping that you will be diagnosed with something that will give them an explanation for your bizarre behaviour.

There is nothing inherently wrong with you. However, your parents and your society do not approve of you. You are labelled as not acceptable by those in authority and your brain is wired to trust and respect those in authority.

Your parent's beliefs and values become your 'ideal-self,' the 'gold standard' self, that you strive to be. Your 'ideal-self' is a psychological construct which is stored in your subconscious (developmental programming). Until this subconscious program is changed, you will experience conflict and tension, because your behaviour is not aligned with your 'ideal-self.' Warning, if unchanged this will remain a tension-causing-issue for your entire life.

Every time you act introverted or are socially awkward, stating facts, you will feel intense discomfort, believing subconsciously, that there is something innately wrong with you and you are not good enough as you are.

Hopefully you can relate in some way to the above example, as it represents a real and common parenting issue, which is present in most families to a lesser or greater degree.

What can you do as a parent to reduce the chance of having a destructive affect upon the development of your child's self-identity?

To recap: the most important two things you can do to be a good parent is to strive to resolve your own developmental issues and challenge your own subconscious false beliefs. Both processes require self-observation and monitoring but cannot be achieved in isolation. You will need support from an independent, impartial person i.e. a counsellor, therapist, psychotherapist or analytical hypnotherapist or life coach.

Once you have you resolved your major issues and removed your significant false beliefs, then you need to be clear what elements of yourself you can and can't change i.e. What you are responsible and accountable for and what you are not.

For example, you are not responsible for your personality, that is a collection of biological and social preferences, which are givens. You are however, 100% responsible and accountable for your character i.e. Your beliefs, values, choices and behaviours. Therefore, this is where most of your focus and effort is best applied. Invest most in what is of most worth and lasts longest i.e. It is where you will get most 'bang for your buck;' most reward for your wise investment.

Once you have achieved this clarity of what you can and can't control, then your eyes will be opened to see what is most important for your child i.e. investing the majority of your time and effort into helping and supporting them to gain clarity regarding what they can and cannot control: helping and supporting them to take 100% responsibility and accountability for the development of their own character.

Below is a list of steps to becoming an 'enlightened parent:'

1. Take full responsibility and accountability for your character (beliefs, values, choices and behaviour)
2. Put your own mental, emotional, social and physical health first. So, you can then be at your best for your children
3. Work through all your developmental issues (whatever developmental issues you do not resolve will be issues or baggage you will pass on to your children)
4. Accept yourself, warts and all
5. Observe your own behaviours in order to identify your false beliefs and replace them with logical, factual beliefs
6. Celebrate your strengths and weaknesses
7. Love yourself for who you are, celebrate yourself
8. Understand child development: physical, psycho-

logical, cognitive, social, emotional and language

9. Understand personality theory

10. Understand your own personality type

11. Think for yourself, do not accept anything as fact unless you can prove it from multiple reliable sources

12. Educate yourself with fact not fable

13. Understand the personality type of your child

14. Accept your child as they are (accepting their psychological preferences as givens)

15. Celebrate your child's innate strengths and weaknesses

16. Help and support your child in the process of them discovering and understanding them self – their psychological preferences and their innate skills

17. Help and support your child to accept them self as they are

18. Teach your child a simple version of the personality theory principles, so they can see for themselves, that everyone is different, and that diversity is not just O.K but something worth celebrating

19. Encourage your child to take responsibility and accountability for their character (beliefs, values, choices and behaviour)

20. Encourage your child to think for them self, and not accept anything as fact unless they can prove it from varying reliable sources

21. Encourage your child to challenge societies established and accepted beliefs and values, to test their validity

22. Encourage and support your child to be self-sufficient and independent

23. Help and support your child to develop the habits of self-discipline required for them to make their dreams come true / lead a fulfilling and productive life

24. Teach your child facts and when you do not know a factual answer or there isn't one, tell them that and explain the different viewpoints and why people have different viewpoints

25. Support your child to become their best self
26. Encourage your child to fully embrace their power to create
27. Encourage your child to make their own decisions, their own path: to create their own life

It is important to remember, we are 'human beings and not human doings,' Rick Warren.

Let me explain further.

Your self-worth, as an adult, doesn't come from anything external as it is generated internally (as mentioned earlier, it is a psychological construct developed as a child and stored as part of your self-identity program in your subconscious – midbrain/limbic system).

Some people strive in vein to obtain self-worth by getting a good-looking partner, an expensive car, a high-flying job or wealth. Self-worth comes from inside. Therefore, your self-worth cannot be obtained from temporary external changes, only by permanent internal changes i.e. Changing the false beliefs in your self-identity program.

In order to establish logic for gauging worth or value, I want to look at how the worth of a saleable product is decided.

It is generally accepted that a product's value is dictated by four factors, three objective and one subjective. I will now explain these four factors below:

1. Rarity – how many are there? Generally, the less there are available the higher the worth i.e. Diamonds
2. Demand – how many people want the item? The more people who want to possess the item the more the item is worth i.e. Diamonds
3. Longevity – how long the item will last? The longer the

life of the item the more it is usually worth i.e. Diamonds

4. Personal value - how much personal value an item has i.e. John Lennon's shoes --- there may have been 30 million of these shoes made. However, because John Lennon wore this pair, an individual who has a significant emotional attachment to John Lennon, may esteem them to be extremely valuable.

Now let's apply this rational thinking to your own self-worth:

1. Rarity – how many of you are there? Well the fact is there's only one of you out of 7.8 billion humans on this planet we call earth. You are unique for your DNA makeup; you have a unique character and a unique selection of experiences. Actually your uniqueness increases even further as you let go of trying to be your 'ideal-self' (doing what you think others want for you) and consciously decide to become your 'real-self,' choosing to do what you think is best.

2. Demand – how many people want you? The demand for you is probably strongest from those who love you most and from those who are dependent upon you i.e. family, friends and work colleagues. It is important to know that as you consciously identify your uniqueness and search the external world to find how your difference can make the biggest difference, demand for you will naturally increase. The world benefits best when you become your 'real-self' and least when you strive to be someone you are not. As your 'real-self' your ability and capacity to serve 'uniquely' increases so the demand for your services correspondingly increases.

3. Longevity – How long will you last? Well that is unknown! However, the part of you which lasts longest is your 'real self,' in other words, your character. Consequently, you will get the greatest return from investing

your time in developing your character in order to become your best self. As you develop your character the value of your service to the world will grow and so will your legacy. Your legacy from the lives you influence for good, lasts forever; passing down from generation to generation.

4. Personal value – how much personal value do you have? Those who love you dearly will view you as priceless as to them you are irreplaceable. This is where it gets even more interesting because humans are different to products: humans have an inherent value whereas products do not. This is because whether a human is liked or not, in demand or not, the worth of a human being is still priceless. Why? Because human potential for good is infinite and is therefore incalculable.

These 1 to 4 value-determining factors above, is a tool you can use, to help you challenge and then modify any false beliefs that underpin your 'developmental self-identity,' which is built upon what you thought significant others wanted you to be.

The diagram below, explains the process of becoming your 'Real self.'

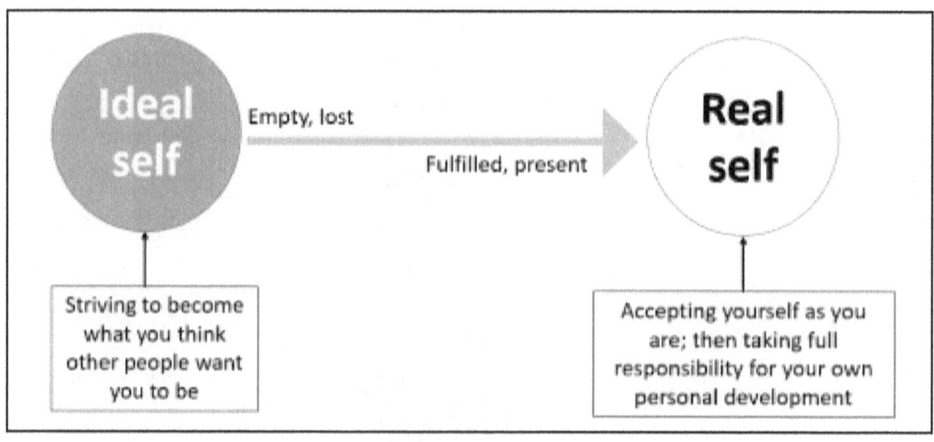

"Your superpower is being yourself," Laura Bushnell

Becoming your 'Real Self' requires conscious effort to fully understand and accept yourself as you are: with your likes, dislikes, strengths, weaknesses, core beliefs, values and your dark side (your dark side being factual things about you that you try and ignore as you falsely believe they are too abhorrent to accept).

It requires identifying and letting go of 'borrowed' beliefs and values and replacing them with your own. It also requires Identifying false-beliefs and replacing them with fact. Lastly, it requires that you identify subconscious fear and hurts, so they no longer hide in the dark but are brought out into the light, where they can be rationally assessed – it is only then, that you realise they are not the big, scary monsters your vulnerable child believed them to be (bringing your dark side into the light). Then you can let the hurt, the pain and fears go, and your emotional scars heal i.e. You will no longer fear people seeing your 'real' self.

A healthy adult, lovingly parents themselves, with two equally strong inner parent voices:

1. The nurturing voice: you can imagine you as an adult giving you as a toddler a big comforting hug and saying, "I love you." In a strong, reassuring voice that effectively comforts you when you make a mistake, saying, "everyone makes mistakes, in fact, it's essential, that's how we learn and grow. I am so proud of your enthusiasm and your progress, well done. Remember, I will al-

ways love you no matter what!"

2. The motivational voice: "It is 7am, go! Get up now! Otherwise you will fall back to sleep. Then you will put unnecessary stress on yourself to get to your 9am meeting. Come on you got this! And at the end of your working day, "Stay strong, you can do this. You've done it before; you'll do it again. One more hour of focus and hard work, that's all, then you've achieved your commitment, and you can treat yourself by going out for tea and playing volleyball with your friends, chin up, head down girl!

If you are constantly feeling stressed and do not feel you are being effective in achieving your dreams, take the time to listen to your inner parenting voices. Are you speaking respectfully to yourself? Are you speaking lovingly to yourself? Are the things you say to yourself motivational or disparaging? A motivational parent inner voice would not put you down or be negative. If your inner parent voices are not speaking to you in a respectful, encouraging and supportive way, then you need to retrain them. Their your voices, you can make them say whatever you want them to say, but it will take at least 2 months of practice to start forming this new habit.

There is no short cut to these developmental issue resolution processes, and it requires taking 100% responsibility and accountability for your own personal development process. Remember, no parent is infallible.

So be patient with yourself and your child and enjoy the journey.

Becoming your 'Real self' is the best thing you can do for yourself and your child. You can then be effective in supporting your child through this process too. Which generally spans the first 40 years of life.

Hence why Carl Jung said, "Life really does begin at 40."

CHAPTER 8: LIFE'S MISSION AND CHARTER

"knowing who you are and what you do for the world gives you purpose. Creating your dream and doing something each day that moves you closer to its fulfilment gives you meaning."

This chapter is about bringing some structure to your self-knowledge so that it can be leveraged optimally to produce the best personal-development results.

I am going to use myself as a template for you to follow.

The information required for the creation of this 'Life's mission and Charter' is all found within the pages of this book. Use below as template for you to build your own.

I am Mark Johnson Joseph

I am an INFJ

My dominant cognitive function is introverted intuition, which is an information gathering and analysing function. Therefore, I am best at gathering and analysing data but not as naturally adept at the decision-making process. My energy is focussed internally.

I am most passionate about creating theories. This comes easily.

I need to make sure I have the alone time necessary each day to wonder and reflect. Walk the dog 3x a day.

My most rewarding challenge, in order that I become more influential and productive, is the healthy development of my extroverted feeling (my 2nd most dominant cognitive function, decision making process).

I need to decide how I create a harmonious situation each day where I can share my theories by written publication and/or by one-to-one coaching/counselling; optimising my impact for good on the lives of others.

Consequently, my primary purpose is:

1. 'I want to wonder & reflect. I am the most reflective of all the personality types.

My secondary dominant cognitive function is extroverted feeling.' Therefore, my secondary purpose is:

2. 'I want to help others and live in peace.'

"As an INFJ, I see my purpose in life is to rescue others, but my real passion is to deep dive to the root cause and permanently fix the underlying issues, so that people never need rescuing again."

Top 3 Character Traits (that inform my life's focus):
1. Altruistic
2. Authentic
3. Wise

My Mission Statement:

"I will utilise my innate motivation to optimise my personal development and help others do the same, by making complex psychological theories simple; so, they can be applied more rapidly and effectively. Creating a more fulfilling world for myself and everyone else, particularly the disadvantaged and vulnerable.

I will regularly use my creativity to write books, that are uplifting, inspiring, humorous and educational, making the world a better place. Helping to lift my self and others out of physical and mental/emotional slavery."

Life motto: "Making the world a brighter place, one book & one coaching session at a time."

Goals:

Each day I will build a growing legacy of:

1. Short concise and simple-to-use, 'Self-development tools,' which will be published as books, for a low a price as possible
2. Psychoanalytical therapeutic practitioner skills, which will include hypnotherapy and neurolinguistic programming techniques

Spending more and more time doing this until I retire in 10 years. At which point I will spend 3.5 days a week doing this work and 3.5 days-a-week doing my fun hobbies and charity work.

Summary of my personality: I am quietly forceful (highly persuasive one-one), original, and sensitive. I tend to stick to things until they are done. I am extremely intuitive about people and sensitive to their feelings. I have a well-developed value system, which I strictly adhere to. I am well-respected for my perseverance in doing what I believe to be the right thing. I am individualistic, I do not desire to lead or follow.

My definition of success: when I have used my very deep understanding of something to do a real service for another. If I am making good progress on my self-development and my intimate relationships are healthy i.e. Those I love most are happy & fulfilled. I am achieving harmony.

Innate Motivation:

Make the future a better and more inspiring place

Altruism & status

Wisdom & expertise

Freedom & autonomy

Fulfil my potential & support others fulfil theirs

Protect the vulnerable

Strengths/weaknesses:

1. *Drive for expertise, innate focus on psychology*
2. *Independent/Individualistic: One to One powerful & profound influence / Poor group facilitator or leader*
3. *Excellent writing skills / Poor verbal communication (both due to dominant cognitive function of introverted intuition)*
4. *Highly emotional/passionate and creative*
5. *Practical dreamer/make vision reality*

Skills I make a living from:

1. Technically minded, good spatial and mechanical aptitude
2. Making complicated processes simple
3. Good technical problem solver – methodical & logical
4. Good attention to technical detail when strategically

required to achieve vision
5. Creative, out of the box thinker

Main Career Focus

1. Now: Technical packaging design - Future-focussed innovation – ecommerce and sustainability
2. Future: Career in Retirement – psychoanalytical therapist/hypnotherapist, life coaching and prolific, eclectic author

Hobbies that I make money from:

1. Psychology – making complicated concepts simple, so I can understand them and explain them succinctly to others – publishing self-help books
2. Creative writing – provocative humour and inspirational stories - publishing books (arranging book signings, which generate funds for travelling, to see my family and the human-made & natural beauty spots around this amazing planet)
3. Personality and character development consultation and coaching

Hobbies that I do for pure fun:

1. Fire – I have a fire table, a stove heated hot tub, fire-pit, campfire, BBQ and outdoor open fire cooking
2. Water– love playing in rivers / lakes (places of stunning natural beauty), jumping in, white water and kayaking
3. Hunting - fishing for trout in small rivers & streams (fair weather fisherman). Watching animals in their natural habitat. BBQ cooking meat.

Giving back – voluntary/charity:

Raising money to support child protection, freedom , education and child-abuse victim support

Romantic Partner Search:

- Female ENTP or ENFP, independent (own house), established career, adventurous (like exploratory outdoor activity, being in nature), 30+ years old. Attractive, healthy, educated, likes dogs & loves music, particularly live music. Ideally got children that have grown up i.e. youngest child being at 10 years of age or older. Looking to have a 'real-love' relationship: where two independent individuals except each other for who they are and enhance each other's lives; supporting and encouraging each other to realise their full potential and dreams

Steps and Rules for Your 'Life's Mission and Charter Creation:'

1. Your personality assessment cannot be done in complete isolation. Once you have carried out the rapid personality test and understand the meaning of each of the 8 psychological preferences. Review your answers with a few people who you trust and who know you intimately and then if you are still in any doubt regarding your personality typing, contact a 'Personality Coach' like myself for expert support. But remember, ultimately it is only you who can work out who you are

2. Use your self-knowledge from 'chapter 4 – Your Life Purpose' to identify your primary and secondary purpose and then use this understanding to create a 'Mission Statement.' A mission statement is a succinct declaration of what you want to achieve in your lifetime

3. Utilise 'Chapter 3: Your Personality Type Traits' tables and the '10-character traits' to work out your innate motivators

4. Refer to 'Chapter 4: Strengths and Weaknesses' to identify your own. Remember, a weakness is the shadow of a strength so-to-speak. For example: the brain wiring which renders me poor at verbal communication is the same wiring that enables my concise and cogent

writing ability. The bigger the weakness, the greater the strength i.e. the bigger the mountain the larger the shadow it casts

5. Your ideal romantic partner information comes from your study of chapter 6

6. All the rest of the Mission Statement and Charter is to be written using your own self-learning. Contact a personality coach, like me, if you would like expert support. My contact details are in the section 'Other Services' later in this book

3 Rules for Successful Personal Development:

1. Do something every day, no matter how small, that moves you closer towards achieving your 'Mission' (5 years away). For example, in 5 years, I will have written 25 books. So, each day I spend a minimum of 30minutes writing a book, with a target of 5 books per year and one book every 2.5 months. Remember, what you do today is the habit that dictates what you will be doing in 5 years. I promise you, if you do something today that brings you closer to completing your mission, you will feel your day and your life is meaningful. It is simple but true.

2. Each day write down two things that are the minimum requirements of your day (they must be genuinely the two most important things and they must be completely realistic). You must complete these two tasks. Prioritise them above everything else, as they are the two most important things. The first task is to do the one thing that will make your life better today and the second task is to do the one thing that will make yours and other people's life better in the future. These two things will give your day a clear purpose and success criteria

3. Make sure, the hobby you can make money from, is something that you absolutely love doing. This is of critical importance. This hobby must come from an innate passion that burns incessantly within you i.e. like writing self-help psychology books does for me. Why? Well it's simply about balance. Because I indulge my passion in my spare time, I have the energy and focus to be successful in my paid career, which frees me up mentally and emotionally to have the time and energy to invest into my hobby. Do you see what this creates? Yes, it is a virtual circle, the one positively feeding the other and you feel energised and fulfilled. It is important to strive for the same level of expertise and achievement through your hobby as you do for your work. The ideal scenario creates a heightened feeling of security, because you know, if your career ended tomorrow you would still have a reasonable living from placing greater focus on your paid hobby. This feeling of security gives you the courage to take more calculated risks during your paid career, which results in greater career success.

Answers for the 12-question quiz in 'Chapter 5: The World Makes More Sense:'

1. Dictatorial, dogmatic organisations i.e. this could mean your Family, religion or society are most likely to view 'Extroverted Perceivers' as rebels or as a threat to their established rules and way of life.

Why? Because a P's psychological preference is to not trust authority, but to be free to find things out from their own experience. Also, because an 'E's' energy is focussed externally, resulting in visible action of speaking out publicly. Their behaviour, which contravenes authority is more likely to be observable.

2. If a relationship is no longer fun, which personality group is most likely to end the relationship? Adventurers

Why? They view a romantic partner as a 'playmate' someone to have fun with. Therefore, if the relationship is no longer fun, their instinctive perception is that the romance has ended.

3. Which personality group is most likely to be devastated if their long-term romantic relationship ends? Dreamers

Why? Because they naturally view a romantic partner as a soul mate

4. If you are talking about how you think our lives will be like in the future, which personality group would be most interested? Dreamers

Why? Their mode of living is the future. Their focus being the generating ideas that will make the future better for everyone.

5. If there is a disaster and you could pick a person to be the leader, which personality group would you want them to be from? Investigators

Why? They are level-headed. Prefer to make decisions based on the facts not emotions. Consequently, they are more likely to make the best decisions that will result in the least fatalities.

6. If you were going on a night out, which personality type would you most want to turn up?

ESFP - Performer

Why? Because they are highly social (EF's) and their strongest desire is to entertain - the life & soul of the party! (SPs – do not want to miss any opportunity for fun and adventure)

7. Which personality type would you pick to organise your wedding?

ESTJ – Supervisor or if you are on a tight budget the ESFJ - Provider

Why? Both are strong organisers (J), who will comfortably deal with all the different people or crowd control (E). Coordinating this complex event effectively and efficiently (SJs, focussed on the 'here & now' great attention to detail, very organised). The ESFJ will more naturally be strong in the area of negotiating the best price if you are on a budget (Conservators – Feelers)

8. If you were feeling depressed which personality type would you speak to?

INFJ - Counsellor

Why? They are individualistic (will put your needs before anything). They are open and empathic. They tend to be wise and genuine people (INFJ– deep thinkers, structuring ideas into wisdom, so they can put individual welfare and development as the top priority). They can see the simple and profound in complicated human predicaments.

9. If you had legal documents that needed filling in, which personality type would you ask to do this task?

ISTJ - Inspector

Why? They have great attention to detail (J). Prefer to make decisions based on fact (T). Highly unlikely to betray your privacy by talking to others (IJs)

10. If you are at the pub and there is a quiz night. Which personality type would you want on your team?

INTJ - Mastermind

Why? Because as their 'descriptor' suggests they have a strong drive to assimilate knowledge (INTJ – deep, global, explorative thinkers that gather and organise important facts, and love to use them to help solve complicated problems)

11. Which personality type is most prone to risk-taking? (you will need to deduct the answer yourself, referring to what you have read so far in this book)

ESTP – Promoter

Why? Because they are hedonistic – seeking pleasure now – love to show off – don't want to miss out on any opportunity for a thrill. Due to having higher testosterone levels, a male ESTP is the most likely to take risks

12. Which 4 personality types are most likely to cheat on their partner? (you will need to deduct the answer yourself, referring to what you have read so far in this book)

ESTP, ESFP, ISFP and ENTP

Why?

It is easy to see why 'Adventurers' would be in this group as they tend to live for the 'here and now' and be hedonistic (require a lot of social interaction and freedom). ENTP's have low tolerance to routine and do not tend to make decisions based on what is generally viewed as 'acceptable' i.e. rules are meant to be broken.

Research shows that extroverts are more likely to cheat. This is ascribed to extroverts being more impulsive, having a stronger desire for variety and being more comfortable socially so having more opportunities.

Bibliography

1. 'Introduction to Psychoanalysis (1917)' By Sigmund Freud
2. 'Psychological Types' (The Collected Works of Carl G. Jung, Vol. 6) (Bollingen Series XX) Paperback – October 1, 1976
3. 'Childhood and Society' Paperback – September 17, 1993 by Erik H. Erikson
4. 'Please Understand Me II: Temperament, Character, Intelligence' (1st Edition) by David Keirsey
5. 'What Type Am I? Discover Who You Really Are' Paperback – August 1, 1998 by Renee Baron
6. "I Surveyed Each Myers-Briggs Type To See Which Type They Were Most Attracted To' – Here Are The Results" by Heidi Priebe, August 16th 2016 - https://thoughtcatalog.com/heidi-priebe/2016/08/i-surveyed-each-myers-briggs-type-to-see-which-type-they-were-most-attracted-to-here-are-the-results/
7. 'The People Puzzle' (1979-07-01) by Morris Massey
8. 'Quiet: The Power of Introverts in a World That Can't Stop Talking' by Susan Cain

Other Services

Please contact me on my mobile 07789033226 or by email Mjjbooks2020@outlook.com

1. If you would like coaching support in the creation of your own unique 'Life's Mission and Charter' document

2. If you would like one to one coaching to gain more insight into your own personality in order to unlock your full potential and achieve a more fulfilling life

3. If you would like one to one coaching to gain more insight into your child's personality or your partners, in order to improve the quality of your intimate relationships

Pay me whatever you think the information I provide is worth.

My Ideal Partner Search

The most important character trait for me is transparency. If you meet the criteria I set out in the last chapter, please contact me by text 07789033226 or by email Mjjbooks2020@outlook.com so we can get to know each other better.

Future Books Like This

Before the end of 2020 I will release the following books on Amazon eBook and paperback:

'Marriage & Divorce Myth Buster' what you wish you had known before getting married or divorced– A hard hitting fact-based study on marriage, which exposes some provocative realities

I am bringing out a 'manual for life' guide for each of the 16 personality types. The first book will be for the ISFJ – dedicated to my oldest son, Adam, again it will be published before the end of 2020

I have also begun writing my first novel, which is a psychological thriller

Other Books I Have Written

Category: Humour

'What Did You Say Again: There is nothing more hilarious and shocking than what our children,' available on Amazon eBook and paperback

ASIN: B084QJT26J

Category: Inspirational

'Dog God Myth: A compilation of inspirational dog stories,' available on Amazon eBook and full-colour paperback

ASIN: B089M2J6KP

Therapeutic Contact Details

John Richardson – 'Psychoanalytical Hypnotherapist'

Email: feelbetterfast@btinternet.com

Tel: 07800 584077

Author Information

I am a 50-year-old father and divorcee, who lives by myself in Batley, West Yorkshire, England. Received my BSC honours degree in Human Communication from Leicester DE Montfort University in 1997.

A large part of my degree was psychology and in the final year of my degree I opted for all psychology modules, majoring in psychology. I am a trained person-centred counsellor and life coach. Am currently enrolled on a 'cognitive therapist' training course and a 'Neurolinguistic training course.' My life-time hobby has been the study of psychology.

By profession I am a packaging developer for a Pet Care blue-chip company. I specialise in pack design for ecommerce and sustainability.

I have two sons (21,17) and two foster daughters (15,10). I am passionate about humour, creativity, adventure and in helping others achieve their full potential.